THROUGH THEIR e_ye_s

THROUGH THEIR e_ye_s

By Welbie D. Houghton

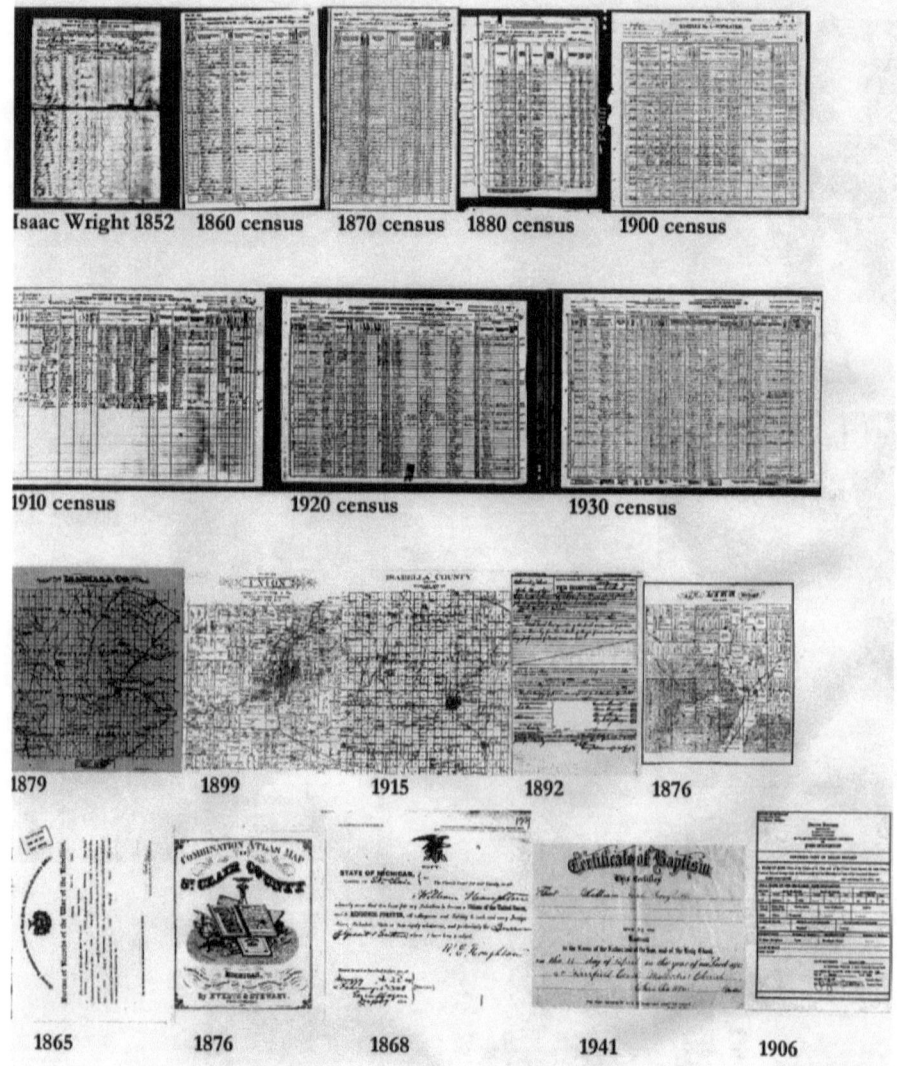

Isaac Wright 1852   1860 census   1870 census   1880 census   1900 census

1910 census   1920 census   1930 census

1879   1899   1915   1892   1876

1865   1876   1868   1941   1906

ISBN 978-0-557-18452-1

THROUGH THEIR e y e s

By

Welbie D. Houghton

Dedication

I come from a hard-working family in a small town that endeavored to live life to the fullest. I learned as a young man that it is much easier to do what God gives me to do, no matter how hard the task is, than to face the accountability of not doing it. I will forever be indebted to grandparents, aunts, uncles, and cousins who have modeled the Christian life. To that conclusion, this book is dedicated to my relatives past, present and future.

Contents

Introduction: Why?

That was the first question I asked myself when I started looking into the history of my family. Why would people sell all their possessions, say good-bye to their families forever, travel four thousand miles over more than three months, and risk their lives and the lives of their loved ones just to subject themselves to further untold hardships and a life in the wilderness?

The many answers to the question "why" have led me to a profound appreciation for my ancestors and everything they endured just to become Americans.

Have you ever tried to see life through someone else's eyes, or tried to feel someone else's experience? This book is an attempt at reliving the lives of my ancestors through the stories handed down from each generation to the next.

A large part of this book is based on firsthand conversations with grandparents, aunts, uncles, cousins, and family friends. There were voluminous amounts of information on the Internet that aided my research tremendously, and information came from many unexpected sources—books, newspapers, and magazines. Many times, it came from strangers who were looking up the history of their own family members, and because a relative of theirs married a relative of mine, they could share stories about my family from their family's perspective.

A lot of information came from my memory; it is amazing what is stored in the recesses of our minds. Oscar Wilde said, "Memory is the diary that we all carry about with us." For instance, I was unsuccessfully trying to memorize the names of the planets in our solar system for my sixth-grade science class when my father nonchalantly said, "**M**y **v**ery **e**ager **m**emory **j**ust **s**eems **u**seful **n**aming **p**lanets." That saying cemented the planets in my memory forever. (They are Mercury, Venus, Earth, Mars, Jupiter, Saturn, Uranus, Neptune, and Pluto.) As I probed my memory for pieces of information about my grandparents, I could actually smell apples as I remembered Grandmother Houghton's kitchen. She had apple trees and often made apple pies or applesauce. When I remembered their living room, I could smell cherry pipe tobacco because my grandfather smoked a pipe.

Before I started research for this book, I had a good idea of what I would find, but there were a great many surprises along the way. This journey has been enlightening, and in many ways I feel I have found some old lost friends. As strange as it may sound, there were times while I was writing this when I felt like I was right there with my relatives as they boarded the ship, got on the stagecoach, walked behind a horse-drawn plow, and built their first log cabin. Catherine Bowne said, "Writing, I think, is not apart from living. Writing is a kind of double living. The writer experiences everything twice. Once in reality and once in that mirror which waits always before or behind."

As I write this book, my branch of the Houghton family has resided in the State of Michigan for 159 years. There have been many changes over that time, but some things remain the same. Names are handed down from one generation to the next, and the exploits of the previous generations are shared with the children. Though some of the names remain the same, the faces to those names have changed, but sometimes only ever so slightly because you can still see the facial features of the older passed on to the younger. One constant will remain: there will always be a great cloud of witnesses cheering the next generation on to success.

It is my wish that each generation remembers and records the deeds of the one before it. May we never forget the sacrifices of our ancestors that made us what we are today, and may we remember to love one another and give God his rightful place in our lives. Go into the world and make your life count for something more than the material. Avoid the rat race at all costs—buying things you do not need, with money you do not have, to impress people you do not like. Be something, live to touch others and be touched by them, live to teach others, and always be open to learn and give, and it will be given to you. You can't touch everyone everywhere, but you can most definitely touch someone somewhere. Most of all, make a difference in your own little part of the world.

Welbie D. Houghton

Never forget those you love. Cherish them, honor them, and remember them often. Share your memories of them, for in doing so they continue to live forever. A man lives as long as he is remembered.

Your tombstone stands among the rest:
Neglected and alone.
The name and date are chiseled out on
Polished marble stone.
It reaches out to all who care
It is too late to mourn.
You did not know that I exist
You died and I was born.
Yet each of us are cells of you.
In flesh, in blood, in bone.
Our blood contracts and beats a pulse
Entirely not our own.
Dear ancestor, the place you filled
One hundred years ago
Spreads out among the ones you left
Who would have loved you so.
I wonder how you lived and loved.
I wonder if you knew
That someday I would find this spot,
And come to visit you.

– Author unknown.

Beginnings

Skegness, Lincolnshire, England
"Perseverance Vincit"

Memories come in several ways: as vivid, multicolored images that include sounds and smells, or as vague, black and white blurred imagery carrying little recollection of the event. Some memories are elastic, and the memory of the event is stretched with each telling; other memories can recreate an event down to the minutest detail. Thankfully, memories can be preserved in writing and photography and can be handed down from generation to generation.

Our earliest memories of family history begin with Great-Great-Great-Grandfather William Houghton. He was born in May of 1792 in the village of Skegness, in the county of Lincolnshire, England. William was a tall man with dark hair and a muscular build. He had no formal education save his training in the military, but he could read and write. He was a virtuous man who taught his children to love God and to be honest and fair.

He joined the British Army in 1811 at the age of nineteen and enlisted in the 49th foot regiment under the command of General Isaac Brock, who was deployed in Canada. His regiment would fight against General Hull of the American forces during the War of 1812. They fought against each other on July 12, 1812 and August  16, 1812, and the British victories in both battles led to the capture of Lake Erie and the Michigan territory. These encounters would introduce young William to the Detroit area, a place he would never forget. At the end of the War in 1815, his regiment returned to England.

After he was discharged from the army, William began tenant farming and well digging in Skegness. Skegness is a harbor town located north of London on the North Sea coast. William met Elizabeth Burns there, and after a short courtship, they were married in 1817.

William paid for his land with his military service, and each year of service gave him five years of land ownership. William received twenty years of land ownership for his four years of service, and then after 1835, when his land ownership ran out, he became a copyholder, which meant he could have his tenancy terminated at any time.

In 1818, William and Elizabeth had their first child and named him William Jr. Their second child, Great-Great-Grandfather John, was born on July 11, 1824 during the first Burmese War between Great Britain and Burma, 1824 to 1826. The war was over land disputes between India, which was a British colony at the time, and Burma's demand for slave labor from India. The war ended in 1826 after a force of just five thousand British troops crushed a Burmese army of sixty thousand. Mary was the third and final child born to William and Elizabeth, but her date of birth is unknown.

Great Britain was the world leader in civil rights in the early 1800s, but there were still areas in need of improvement. William Sr. tells a story of his friend Clive, who was an attorney subjected to pillory in 1829. Clive was found guilty of encouraging a witness to give false testimony at a trial in which he was involved. He received five years' imprisonment in an Australian penal colony and had to endure two hours of public humiliation on the pillory. The attorney's ears were nailed to the wooden frame of the pillory to prevent him from moving his head, and then he was pelted with rotten vegetables for two hours. The pillory was outlawed in Great Britain in 1837.

John Houghton and Jane Sleight met at an early age because they grew up just a quarter-mile from one another. They attended the same school and church and often talked to one another at both. John would pull Jane's ponytail, and she would kick him in the shins. When other boys picked on her, he would defend her, and they would walk home from school together. They never officially said they liked each other but the signs where there.

One summer's day when John was twelve, he and Jane spent the afternoon at John's favorite fishing hole. Jane pretended that she was afraid to bait the hook and made John do it for her. When she caught a fish, she also made John remove the fish from the hook. They teased one another, and John told funny stories that made Jane laugh. They talked about their likes and dislikes and found that they had quite a lot in common. As they talked, John would get lost in Jane's warm blue eyes and forget what they were talking about. John had a splinter in his finger, and when Jane saw it, she touched his hand and drew it close to her to get a good look at the splinter. John never realized how soft and elegant

Jane's hands were. As Jane studied John's hand, John just studied Jane's face. He saw the concern and compassion in her eyes as she tried to remove the splinter from his finger. When it was time for them to leave, John said good-bye, stole a kiss from Jane, and then ran all the way home. From that moment onward, Jane knew John was the boy she would someday marry.

Later that summer, Jane's parents moved the family to a town three days by horse from Skegness. Jane realized the significance of the move and tried to see John one last time before they left, but she never got the opportunity. Jane had several suitors while they were separated, but she knew in her heart that someday she and John would get back together.

In 1837, shortly after Jane's family moved, John became an apprentice chimney sweep at the age of thirteen and worked the job until he turned sixteen in 1840. As a chimney sweep, John was well liked and considered lucky because in England it was good luck to shake hands with a chimney sweep or have him blow a kiss at you. In 1840, he had to give up the job when the Chimney Sweep Act was passed prohibiting employment of children under the age of twenty-one as chimney sweeps.

Also that year a close family friend died and William used the circumstances to make clear to his family the facts of death, existing, and truly living. He told them there were thousands of ways a person can die, but there was only one way a person could really live. You could spend your life in the pursuit of accumulating things that would not bring any lasting dividends, or you could invest your life in the Kingdom of God and reap eternal rewards. A life lived for Jesus Christ would bring joy and happiness now and in heaven. A life lived for you and the world's treasures would bring emptiness and regret.

William's talk took place just before John's sixteenth birthday. John had been to church all his life, listened to his father and mother pray and even read the family bible, but he only did it because it made his father and mother happy. He had knowledge of God and Jesus, but there wasn't any personal relationship of his own.

William spoke for several minutes, and every word he said pierced John's heart. This moment was unlike any other time in John's life. When William spoke, John's spiritual eyes and ears were opened for the first time; he heard the truth, and the truth was setting him free. John asked his father to pray with him to dedicate his life to Jesus. William began to pray, and for the first time in John's life, he wished his father's prayer would never stop. Before that day, he had endured his father's prayers, but now, he was enthralled by them.

After praying with John, William told him that he must be baptized and read the Bible everyday. John could understand reading the Bible, but what did baptism have to do with anything? William told John that baptism was an outward sign of an inward work. It was like washing away the old self and emerging from the water a brand-new person dedicated to God. John was baptized the following Sunday.

John didn't own a Bible, but wanted one so badly that his soul began to cry out to God for wisdom how to get one. He was consumed with the desire to read the word of God. One day while at the market square, John ran into an old friend he hadn't seen for some time. After talking to him for a while, the friend's father approached John and unexpectedly asks John if he would like to work on his farm for a few months. Without hesitation, John immediately said, "Yes." John later thanked God for answering his prayer. He now had two jobs and was able to buy the Bible after many months of working long hours. Bibles were expensive in 1840, but God arraigned a chance meeting with someone who had a used Bible for sale. John bought that Bible, and to him it was worth more than life itself.

William Jr. got married and had five children. The name of William's wife is unknown, but their children's names were:

1.   Maryann (1836)

2.   Betsy (1839)

3.   Rebecca (1842)

4.   William (1845)

5.   Mariah (1846)

Great Britain was improving the standard of living for its citizens and continued to pass laws that made life tolerable for everyday people. In 1844, it passed the Factory Act, which made life a little easier for working women and children. The law imposed a maximum twelve-hour workday for women and a maximum six-hour workday for children six to thirteen years old.

Many years passed, and John hadn't heard anything about Jane; he kept himself occupied with chores on his father's farm. Then one evening John was informed by his older brother that the Sleight family had moved back to the area and was planning a social gathering to reunite with old friends. It was no accident that the Houghtons were invited to the party.

The night of the party was on midsummer, and everyone was outside standing around a campfire taking turns poking at the fire and watching specs of red ash float into the dark, windless night. The  air was cool and filled with the sounds of summer; there wasn't a cloud in the sky.

John was busy poking at the fire when he glanced across the campfire and caught Jane staring at him, and she smiled. He immediately looked down at the fire, then shyly looked back at her and saw that she was still smiling at him. John knew that sometime in his long ago, Jane had held a place in his heart, and seeing her tonight began to stir up those old feelings. Then, as if lightning had struck him, his eyes were opened for the first time... she had been right there in front of him nearly all his life, but he never really saw her as he did tonight. She looked stunning; the way the light from the campfire illuminated her feminine curves and her captivating smile made John lose all his inhabitations. He strolled over to her side of the campfire, they started to talk, and he knew immediately in his heart that she was the one for him.

After that night, they began to see one another on a regular basis. John said that Jane made him a better person, and she made him experience emotions he had never felt before. Jane's intuition had told her from that first stolen kiss that John was the one she would someday wed. They completed one another; Jane's strengths complimented John's weaknesses, and Jane's beauty blinded John to any limitations Jane might have had. John was ready to get married and disliked saying good-bye to Jane every night. John was spellbound by Jane's beauty and often told her, "I hate to see you leave, but I love to watch you go."

Great-Great-Grandfather John married Jane Sleight in 1845 at the age of twenty-one. John was of medium build and muscular, with long blond hair. He had a chiseled face and light blue eyes. He perpetually had a farmer's tan, earned from working outside all day. John had received some formal education and was wise beyond his schooling. He was honest, and people knew that his handshake was better than a contract.

Jane (Sleight) Houghton, born on March 20, 1819, was the daughter of Shadrach Sleight. Jane was of slender build, with long flowing curly brown hair. She had fair skin and a smile that could melt the hardest of hearts. John often remarked that he regularly got lost in her warm blue eyes. Jane was strong-willed but not overbearing, industrious and hardworking, but she understood what the French call *joie de vie*, the joy of living. She greeted everyone with open arms and extended her hands to the needy. Her love for God governed how she lived.

* * *

John and Jane had seven children together. Three children were born in England, and four were born in America. The names of the children born in England were:
1.   Great-Grandfather John (May 11, 1846) – Lincolnshire

2.   Eliza (March 31, 1848 to January 10, 1921) – Lincolnshire

3.   Emma (1850) – Lincolnshire

John and his older brother William both worked with their father, tenant farming and well digging. They made a good living doing what they did, but they yearned for more. They wanted to own their own land and have a better future for their children. Two things concerned them at the time: firstly, the fact that they were tenant farmers and could be thrown off their land at any time, and secondly, that the potato famine in Ireland, which began in 1845, was putting a burden on everyone to get food. They were seriously considering many options but had not decided on any specific one.

Epiphany

Fall 1849

What they feared the most happened again. This was the second well collapse within a year, and now William Sr. was trapped beneath a ton of earth. William Jr. and John dug frantically to free their father. The wooden supports used to hold the well's sides and prevent a cave-in partially protected him from suffocation. The boys freed him just in time, and William had cheated death a second time.

As the boys pulled William from his sarcophagus, he took a big gulp of fresh air and all three of them collapsed on the ground exhausted. After a short period of rest, all three men got to their knees and the boys thanked God for saving their father's life.

The boys said that William changed that day; he said one of the most eloquent prayers they had ever heard. This was a life-changing moment, when the past became irrelevant and everything was new. Freedom from the well and certain death caused William to have an epiphany. He wasn't just liberated from the well but from everything that had held him back in his life. He saw everything more clearly than he had ever seen before. It was as though he had revelatory vision, and the unimportant things of life had disappeared, leaving only what mattered the most.

After he talked to his boys about his experience, they decided to allow God to live large inside them. They knew that if they delighted themselves in the Lord, He would give them their heart's desires. Their decision was to take their chances and come to America, specifically to the newly formed state of Michigan. William had never forgotten the beautiful land and lakes he had seen there during his time in the army. The allure of owning their own land and providing a better life for their families far outweighed the rigors and dangers of moving to the unknown. William told the boys, "Cowards die a thousand deaths. The valiant taste of death but once," a quote from his favorite compatriot, William Shakespeare.

The men told their wives about their experience and what they felt God was leading them to do. At first the women were hesitant, but they eventually warmed to the idea, and before the men left for America they were excited about the adventure on which they were about to embark.

They began to plan their move and learned all they could about travel to America. The first thing they learned was that the trip would be long, exhausting, and require every ounce of strength they could muster. They knew that without God's help they might not make the journey successfully, so they made a conscious decision to invoke God's guidance in every aspect of their planning. William quoted one of his favorite proverbs from the Bible: "Trust in the Lord with all your heart and lean not on your own understanding, in all your ways acknowledge him and he will direct your paths."

The planning phase rapidly moved to the implementing phase, and now it was time to put the information into action.

Coming to America

1850

In May 1850, William, now fifty-eight, William Jr., thirty-two, and John, twenty-six, traveled from Skegness to Waterloo Dock in Liverpool, England to board the ship *Emigrant,* which was headed to New York. They left behind William's wife, Elizabeth, and daughter Mary, who was now married. Also left behind were the families of William Jr. and John. They would send for their families when they had settled in America.

The children were apprehensive about being apart from their fathers for such a lengthy time. To help comfort them, the men told the family to look for the North Star every night and speak to it as if they were having a conversation with them. The star would remind the children that the men were thinking of them. John informed the children that the North Star was an unswerving constant that would always direct them to true north, just as their love would always direct the men to them.

The trip from Skegness to Liverpool would be a combination of stagecoach and train travel. There were no direct routes by train to Liverpool from Skegness, and because they had to travel a convoluted path, it was over 350 miles to their destination. The 1844 Railway Act in Great Britain set the cost of riding the train at a penny a mile.

When the men arrived at the Waterloo dock, they were greeted by a carnival atmosphere. There were vendors selling anything imaginable. They were propositioned several times by women of the night and were nearly sold tickets to a nonexistent ship. They also had to keep a watchful eye out for the skilful pickpocket, one of which nearly absconded with William Jr.'s wallet. After several queries and cautious investigation, William Sr. purchased their tickets for the voyage at a cost of four pounds a person. William showed the tickets to the boys, and they looked intently at them like they were made of gold. In William's hands lay the tickets to their hopes and dreams for a better future.

Before boarding the ship, they had to undergo a medical inspection by a government-appointed surgeon. He would not allow anyone with an infectious disease to board the ship. This inspection was cursory and consisted of the following: "What is your name? Are you well? Hold out your tongue; all right, next."

Included in the price of the ticket was weekly provision for each emigrant. These included two and a half pounds of bread, a pound of wheat flour, five pounds of oatmeal, two pounds of rice, two ounces of tea, half a pound of sugar, half a pound of molasses and vinegar, a pound of pork, and three quarts of water a day. They would have to do their own cooking during the voyage. The men brought their own cooking utensils, tin ware, bedding, and towels.

During the voyage, they endured many hardships. The ship's crew was notoriously brutal to the emigrants. There was little food, and it was never given as prearranged. They had to battle seasickness, storms, sleep deprivation, homesickness, and boredom.

Finally, the ship was towed from the dock and out to sea. The voyage had now begun. It was now that the eyes of the emigrants began to shed tears as they waved good-bye to their homeland, the home of their fathers and the country of their childhood. As those aboard the ship watched the shoreline disappear, you could hear them sing...

Far away oh Far away

We seek a world o'er the ocean spray

We seek a land across the sea

Where bread is plenty and men are free

The sails are set, the breezes swell

England our country

Farewell Farewell

1850 sailing route – England to New York

Lynn, Michigan
The Beginning 1850-1852

The voyage would take six weeks in all, and there are few details about what transpired on the trip across the Atlantic. We do know that someone was murdered during the trip. The killer was then convicted in a trial in New York and hanged before the men left for Michigan. Their ship reached New York harbor in the middle of June, and their final destination would be Lynn, Michigan, but before they could take the stagecoach, they needed to improve their finances with a little employment. The men got jobs in New York City and worked there for three months before continuing on their journey.

They did several odd jobs while in the city, including working at a slaughterhouse. There were over two hundred slaughterhouses in the city, and over 375,000 animals were slaughtered every year. This job was demanding, incredibly grueling, and one they could only stomach for two weeks before finding other employment.

With only rudimentary sanitation, New York City was a health disaster waiting to happen. One year before the men arrived, the city had a cholera outbreak that killed over five thousand people.

The men stayed at a boarding house on Chamber Street, not far from the almshouse. It was located on the edge of the neighborhood known as Five Points, a district known for thieves, drunkards, and other unseemly characters. Many a night while the men were there, they would wake to the noise of a drunken brawl in the streets. They always made it a habit to stay together at all times to look out for one another.

Their time in New York wasn't all work, and they were even able to attend a Jenny Lind performance at the Castle Garden. Jenny Lind, known as the Swedish Nightingale, was a singing phenomenon from Europe. P. T. Barnum brought her to America and she started her two-year American tour on September 11, 1850 in New York City. The men attended a sold-out performance on September 12, 1850. She sang songs by Bellini, Rossini, Weber, and Meyerbeer, and she performed an encore by Stephen Foster.

The men began their trip for their new home in Michigan in October of that year. The stagecoach trip to Lynn was over 650 miles. On an average day they could travel just twenty miles, and even fewer when climbing through the hills. The roads were rough, and in many places just the tracks of the wagon wheels let you know that you were still on the trail. In 1850, a forty-day journey from New York to Michigan was considered high-speed travel.

They arrived in Lynn, Michigan on November 22, 1850, and John bought 160 acres in January 1851. The new-land law passed in 1820 set the price of land at $1.25 an acre, so John's land cost him two hundred dollars. William Sr. bought eighty acres that he later gave to John.

The men began to clear the land and spent the first harsh winter living in a tent. The main homestead of 160 acres was mostly flat. Mill Creek, which ran through the north end of the property, was so clear you could see a pebble in eight feet of water, and the land where they planted crops was rich and fairly easy to cultivate.

William knew how to use his rifle and was an excellent marksman, a skill he would pass to the younger Houghtons over the years. There was plenty of wild game in the area to keep the men fed. They recall how pleasant and full-flavored their first white-tailed deer tasted, especially after so many weeks of eating hardtack. They also feasted on elk, squirrel, turkey, goose, rabbit, bear, and fish.

They would spend long twelve-hour days cutting trees and pulling stumps to clear the land for farming. They bought two mules, Bessie and Harry, to do the lion's share of the plowing and stump pulling on the farm. They would also have to build homes and outbuildings, dig wells, and buy livestock, all while clearing the land, planting crops, and looking for food on a daily basis.

St Clair County, Michigan. Lynn Township, upper left-hand corner.

Life was extremely tough that first winter. The men had never experienced weather so cruel and austere. Some nights when the wind was blowing against their tent, the temperature could get as cold as twenty below. The men had to keep mentally sharp at all times just to stay alive. There were no doctors in the region, so they had to depend upon God to keep them healthy. As if the hard life in the wilderness was not enough, they had to battle the loneliness of missing their loved ones back in England.

They fondly recall their first Christmas in Michigan. Their day started by digging through two feet of snow that had fallen on their tent during the night. The entire countryside had a thick blanket of fluffy white snow that was so beautiful it almost made them forget their freezing fingers and toes. They started a fire with flint and steel and cooked fresh venison from a deer that William Sr. had shot the day before. They also ate a cake of hard bread with some bean soup and stewed corn. To top everything off, they had a can of fine oysters, which they had brought along just for the occasion. They ate their food around the campfire and

reminisced about life back in England. They finished their meal with a hot cup of tea and relaxed, huddled next to the warm fire.

They were invited to a neighbor's home for a Christmas meal in the afternoon. The home was about a mile's walk through the woods, and they started out at about one in the afternoon. While they were walking, it began to snow big, fat, fluffy white flakes that gently floated down from the sky and added another layer to the winter mantle on the ground. It was slow going, treading through the thick snow, and they had worked up a large appetite by the time they finally reached their neighbor's cabin.

They had a large meal together, and then the woman of the house read a Hans Christian Anderson story called *The Little Match Girl*. The story is about a poor little girl forced to sell matches on the streets of New York City on New Year's Eve. The little girl knows that if she does not sell any matches, her brutish, cruel father will beat her when she returns home.

As the night progresses, the little girl gets cold from the bitter winter air and begins to light the matches to keep warm. In the glow of the lit matches, she sees visions, first of a Christmas tree, then of a holiday feast. She looks toward the sky and sees a falling star; her dead grandmother told her that a falling star meant that someone was dying. She lights another match and sees her dead grandmother, the only person in her life who ever showed her any love and kindness. The little girl begs her grandmother to take her with her, and the next morning, passersby find the little girl lying dead in the street, smiling.

When they were done discussing the fairy tale, everyone took turns sharing stories about themselves and their families. John talked about his family and how he missed them so much he ached. He told everyone about his beautiful wife, Jane, and how he felt warm inside every time he thought about her. He had started to share a personal story about his wife when his emotions caught up with him. He became quiet, hung his head, and then wiped the tears from his eyes. He regained his composure and continued to tell everyone about the love of his life, his beautiful wife. He said that he needed her more than he needed food; without her, his life had no meaning, and she was the reason he got out of bed every morning. He believed that he became the most blessed man in the world the day Jane married him, and King Solomon's riches did not measure up to the wealth she brought to his life.

William Sr. talked about his wife, Elizabeth. They met at the market square in Skegness shortly after William had been discharged from the army. Elizabeth was selling produce from her father's farm. William did not need or even want what she was selling, but he did want to talk to her. By the time he was done conversing with her, he had bought nearly everything she had brought to market that day. He said that Elizabeth was beautiful, with light, strawberry-red hair, and fair skin. She was half-Irish and spoke with an Irish brogue. Elizabeth was full of life, kind and generous, but when she was angered, she had a temper that matched her red hair. Elizabeth wanted a large family, but after her miscarriage of their fourth child, she never got pregnant again. William said she was a good mother and loving wife.

It was so comfortable and warm in the cabin the men almost forgot about the winter outside. The fluffy snowflakes turned into an intense, heavy snowstorm just after they got to the cabin and continued into the night. When it was time for the men to leave, they opened the door and discovered thirteen inches of fresh snow already on the ground with a blistering wind. Their neighbors convinced them to spend the night, which they humbly and thankfully did.

Lynn was a dangerous wilderness when they arrived; it teemed with wolves and bears, and even the livestock was vulnerable when left unattended. The men found many opportunities to make money from the abundance of wild animals they had never encountered before. Each new day brought innovative ways to deal with the wildlife.

One day they awoke to find wolves stealing the last of their game they had cleaned and stored in the snow. There was an eleven-dollar bounty on wolves, so the men decided to earn some badly needed money while thinning the wolf population. There were so many wolves in the area that the men were able to earn enough money to buy more supplies and some farm animals in the spring. They also trapped several dozen muskrats and traded the hides to get most of their staples for the year.

Times were changing in America. In 1850, the United States added another star to its flag with the addition of California as a state.

The official flag was not introduced until July of 1851. The flag was thirty-one stars strong for now, but trouble was brewing because in ten short years those stars would be tested as never before during the Civil War. Three other stars were added to the United States in 1850: not stars you could see on the flag, but earthbound stars named William, William Jr., and John.

The men worked hard building a log cabin that first year. It was five rooms of rustic bliss--with no running water or flush toilets. The cabin had knotty cedar-log walls chinked with wedge-shaped strips of wood and plastered with clay. Occasional cracks in the chinking allowed air and small creatures into the cabin. The ceiling was open, with a loft across the back half of the cabin. This made the cabin feel larger than it actually was. Three Spartan bedrooms and a small kitchen lined the outside wall of the cabin. In the center of the cabin was a large, homey living room. At one end of the living room was a majestic fieldstone fireplace with an oak hearth. On the wooden floor in front of the fireplace was a large black bear rug. John had killed the bear during their first winter at Lynn. John Jr. spent many nights growing up dreaming about fighting and slaying that bear. Some nights he won and other nights he just woke up.

Building a farm from the ground up was new to the men. There were times when they faced a problem so multifaceted that they studied it until the stars were lost in the light of day. The men labored indefatigably every day on the farm, stopping only on Sundays to worship their God. They knew that the harder they worked, the sooner their families could join them. They worked from sunup to sundown, in good weather and bad, to make their farms fit for human habitation. Taking a day off when they did not feel good was not an option to them. They were inspired by the thoughts of their families and anything that would help bring them to America more rapidly.

The first year swiftly passed and they were astonished at the improvement they had made on the farm. They now had a residence with some outbuildings, a working well, and eighty acres of tillable land. With the help of their neighbors, they put up their barn during their second winter at Lynn. The winter was manageable now that they had a roof over their heads and a warm fire in the cabin.

The second winter was kind to them and they were able to accomplish many required duties on the farm. Now with spring coming, the men felt that it was safe for their families to join them. They wrote a letter to their loved ones notifying them that it was time to make the journey to America. They prayed over the letter, put their families in God's hands, and sent the letter to England. Now all they could do was wait.

A Death, a Refusal, and Saying Good-bye

Once settled in Lynn in 1852, the men sent for their families. William Jr.'s wife had died soon after William left England. Elizabeth, wife of elder William, elected to stay in England with her married daughter, Mary, and never came to America. Elizabeth was about sixty years old by now, and the rigors of the ocean crossing, the stagecoach trip, and pioneer life in general appeared too formidable for her. Elizabeth struggled with her decision to stay in England right up to the moment it was time to leave. Ultimately, her uncertainties got the better of her.

This left John's wife, Jane, age thirty-three, to care for her own three children and the five motherless children of William Jr. Jane enlisted the help of her younger sister, Eliza Sleight, to help bring the eight children to America. Jane's three children were young: John Jr. was six; Eliza, four; and Emma, two. William Jr.'s children were Maryann, sixteen; Betsy, thirteen; Rebecca, ten; William III, seven; and Mariah, six.

Before they could leave, Jane had the formidable task of selling the remainder of the family possessions and getting the children ready for the long, arduous trip ahead of them. Saying good-bye to Elizabeth,

Mary, and the Sleight family was bittersweet. Jane understood she would never see them again, but a new life and reuniting with John took a little heartache out of the separation.

Jane's father, Shadrach, drove everyone in his wagon to the station. Shadrach was a peaceful, tenderhearted man who loved his two daughters more than anything he had ever loved in his entire life. He especially loved Jane, doted over her, and looked forward to being a grandfather as a prize deserved by an older parent. He cherished his

time with Jane and loved being with his grandchildren, and now everything he had waited for was being taken from him. He was losing both daughters—the only children he had. It felt as though someone was ripping his heart from his chest, and it took every ounce of courage he could muster to let them go. At one point, he considered begging them to stay, but ultimately he put them into God's hands and gave them his blessing.

He purposely slowed the team of horses as they rode to the station; he wanted to spend as much time with Jane and his grandchildren as he could. He was hoping for a miracle—maybe Jane would come to her senses, change her mind on the way to the station and stay in England. Every fiber in his body resented this ride and the consequences it would bring. He knew this ride to the station would be the last time he would ever see them, and they would no longer be a part of his life.

He thought about his daughter's life and the milestones she had passed as she grew up: her birth, her first steps, the first time she helped her mother cook, her first day at school, her wedding day, and then the birth of her first child. He especially loved the early years of Jane's life, when he was the only man in her life. She looked to him for all the answers, and in her eyes he could do no wrong. Shadrach's own eyes began to moisten as he remembered different events he shared with his daughter.

Jane was aware of what her father was going through because she was experiencing similar feelings. She saw the tears in her father's eyes and slid close to him, put her arm around him and said, "I love you, Papa."

They both quietly cried together, and then Shadrach said in a low tone so no one else could hear, "We must be strong for the children. I want to remember you smiling. You know I've always loved your stunning smile."

At last they arrived at the station, and Shadrach helped everyone unload their luggage from the wagon and onto the stagecoach. The family stood nervously waiting for the driver to tell them when to board the coach. No one said a word, and they stood like statues as the coachman counted the group and then directed everyone to get on the carriage. Each person hugged Shadrach one last time before climbing aboard the coach. Shadrach looked intently at each of his family, studying his or her face before finally saying good-bye. He was imprinting a mental photo, and to him everyone would remain the way they looked that day, eternally young.

They were on their way, and Shadrach became smaller and smaller as they traveled from the station. Jane kept up a courageous face, smiled and waved at her father until he was out of sight, and then cried as she had never cried before. Her sobbing was mixed with, "I love you, Papa, Keep safe, and God bless."

Shadrach watched the coach until it disappeared from sight, climbed into his wagon, and made the long, lonely ride back home. He was inconsolable for weeks after they left and often remarked that the day was more like a funeral than any interment he had ever attended.

Jane, Eliza, and the children first had to travel across England from Skegness to Liverpool. After a few days' travel, they eventually arrived in Liverpool. Liverpool was a large metropolis and a harbor port that was the starting point for many emigrants. The city was the second largest in England at that time, with over 352 thousand people in 1852. Many people in Liverpool made their living from the shipping industry, and the unscrupulous made theirs separating the emigrant from his money. Neither Jane nor Eliza had ever been to a big city before, so they were extra-vigilant and not as trusting as they would have been back home.

Once in Liverpool, Jane had to watch for the streetwise con men and racketeers that plundered the emigrant at every stage and step of the emigration process. Before they could get on their ship, they had to deal with shipbrokers, boardinghouse keepers who overcharged them, and provision stores who sold them bad food and drink at high prices. Jane learned very quickly how to play the game. She was as gentle as a dove but as shrewd as a serpent. They ended up with additional items for the trip simply because of Jane's bargaining skills and her ability to stretch a dollar. One item Jane was able to purchase with her extra money was blankets. Everyone had their own blanket, and there were many cold nights during the trip that they were so thankful for it.

They stayed at Marshalls Hostel at an expense of four pence a night for each person. This included bedding, blankets, writing paper, a hot bath, and a fire for cooking. They had to spend five nights at their hostel before boarding the ship. Jane, Eliza, and the children made a group of ten and were quite the sight when they were in public because Jane made everyone hold hands while they were walking the streets. The youngest two usually had to be carried because they had a difficult time keeping up with everyone.

The children were amazed at the sights of the city and were beginning to realize there was an enormous world outside of Skegness. Up to now, their only exposure to the outside world was through reading books, and at this moment, the books were coming to life. They were taking in every experience like sponges and could barely wait for each new day's adventure.

Jane arranged passage to America at the Charles Hill Company on one of the Black Ball Line ships called the *Isaac Wright*. Charles Hill was a merchant and shipbroker located at 60 Waterloo Road, which ran directly in front of Waterloo Dock. The cost of the ticket was three pounds ten shillings ($17.50 US).

Passengers were permitted to board the ship one night before sailing, and on May 17, 1852, the family met at Waterloo Dock, went through the medical inspection, and finally boarded the ship to America. There was a good stiff wind on the morning of the 18th as they set sail for New York Harbor with a total of 533 other passengers on board the *Isaac Wright*.

A steamer towed the ship down the river and out to sea, staying with the ship until all passengers were checked and the ship was cleared of stowaways. If any stowaways were found on board, they would be lowered to the tugboat and taken back to shore. The captain had to ensure the proper number of passengers were on the ship because he risked a fine of fifty dollars and one year in prison for each passenger carried over the permitted number.

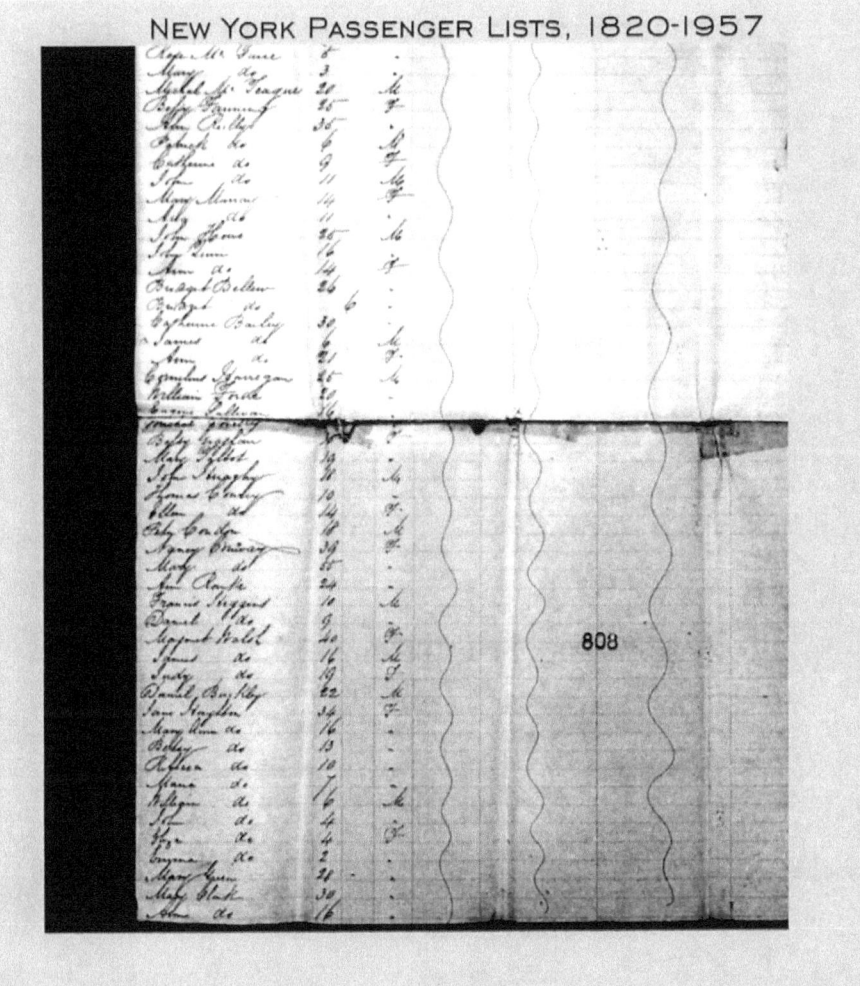

NEW YORK PASSENGER LISTS, 1820-1957

JANE HOUGHTON

ARRIVAL DATE: 24 JUN 1852
ESTIMATED BIRTH YEAR: ABT 1818
AGE: 34
GENDER: FEMALE
PORT OF DEPARTURE: LIVERPOOL, ENGLAND
DESTINATION: UNITED STATES OF AMERICA
PLACE OF ORIGIN: UNITED STATES OF AMERICA
ETHNICITY/RACE/NATIONALITY: AMERICAN
SHIP NAME: ISAAC WRIGHT
PORT OF ARRIVAL: NEW YORK
LINE: 44
MICROFILM SERIAL: M237
MICROFILM ROLL: M237_115
LIST NUMBER: 808
PORT ARRIVAL STATE: NEW YORK

SOURCE INFORMATION: WWW.ANCESTRY.COM DATABASE: NEW YORK PASSENGER LISTS, 1820-1957 DETAIL: YEAR: 1852; ARRIVAL: , ; MICROFILM SERIAL: M237; MICROFILM ROLL: M237_115; LINE: ; LIST NUMBER: .

Jane and children near the bottom of page. Last name spelled 'Houghton'.
June 24, 1852

JANE HOUGHTON

ARRIVAL DATE: 24 JUN 1852
ESTIMATED BIRTH YEAR: ABT 1818
AGE: 34
GENDER: FEMALE
PORT OF DEPARTURE: LIVERPOOL, ENGLAND
DESTINATION: UNITED STATES OF AMERICA
PLACE OF ORIGIN: UNITED STATES OF AMERICA
ETHNICITY/RACE/NATIONALITY: AMERICAN
SHIP NAME: ISAAC WRIGHT
PORT OF ARRIVAL: NEW YORK
LINE: 44
MICROFILM SERIAL: M237
MICROFILM ROLL: M237_115
LIST NUMBER: 808
PORT ARRIVAL STATE: NEW YORK

The *Isaac Wright* – Black Ball Line 1852

Jane and the Children Come to America

The Voyage
1852

The captain of the ship was Edward G. Furber. He was a forty-two-year-old Englishman who had spent all but the first twelve years of his life at sea. Edward worked his way up the ladder by performing the many duties as a seaman until he became the captain of the ship. He knew everyone's job on the ship forwards and backwards because he had done them all himself over the years.

He was a salty, rough-spoken man with a patch over his left eye that made him look like a pirate-ship captain. The patch had been earned in a drunken brawl over a Frenchwoman when he was a young man. He lost an eye as well as the woman in the scuffle and often remarked, "The wench wasn't worth one speck of me eye, let alone me whole eye." He was a portly man with a large, rotund belly that bounced up and down when he laughed, but he seldom did because he was all business and determined to get the ship to New York in record time.

Now aboard the ship, Jane and Eliza had the daunting task of keeping the children fed, healthy, and safe. The long days of monotony aboard the ship were broken only by the sheer terror of the battering sea storms. Their Bible and strong faith in God was the solid rock that got them through the many trials along the way.

The constant rocking of the ship leading to seasickness was soon replaced by sea legs. One trick Jane used to help the children get over seasickness was sucking on a lemon.

There was little privacy on the ship; it was only 175 feet long, 22 feet deep, and 33 feet wide, and it had two decks. Except for the captain's quarters, the crew's quarters, and the lockable storage rooms for the ships provisions, everything else on the ship was open. The passengers slept in an open bay on long planks of wood three or four people across. Every morning the captain and shipmates would make all passengers get out of bed and clean out their sleeping area. This helped reduce the amount of sickness and disease on the ship. They also had to use a chamber pot to go the bathroom and throw the contents overboard when done. The sleeping quarters had a peculiar odor that could be expected from housing over five hundred people with little ventilation and no bathing facilities. The odor became more pungent the longer the voyage went on.

Everyone was responsible for cooking their own food, and the ship had only ten cooking stations on board for over five hundred people. Many times during the voyage, the children would have to wait long periods before they could cook their next meal. They would become impatient as they waited, and Jane would remind them of a maxim that she was taught when she was a young woman: "Patience is a virtue, virtue is a grace, put them both together and you have a pretty face."

In the morning, every passenger was given three quarts of water for the day. Jane would ration the water to the children throughout the day, and at the end of the day, if there was enough water left, they could wash their bodies before they went to sleep.

Jane could read and write and used the time aboard the ship to tutor the children. She had a copy of the Bible and Dilworth's spelling book, and each child took turns reading from the books and spelling out the words. She would begin each day with a proverb from the Bible to impart wisdom to the children, and then a psalm to gain knowledge of praise and thankfulness.

The voyage wasn't all bad. There were nights when the moon was full, and Jane and the children would sit on the deck, gaze into the heavens and watch falling stars. The view was intoxicating and led to many conversations about what might lie beyond those stars. They would always examine the sky for the North Star, and when they found it, they would have a discussion about their  fathers. When they were done talking, they would say, "Good night, Papa." The nights when the ocean was calm and had a slight breeze were the best because the gentle rocking of the ship induced precious sleep.

The book *Moby Dick* was published the year before they boarded the ship and had become an instant success. The children had heard the story while they were still in England and earnestly looked for the great white whale while at sea. Every time there was a storm, they were afraid the ship would capsize and the whale would eat them. The children made the mistake of telling two crewmembers about the tale of Moby Dick and the two taunted the children for the remainder of the journey with false sightings of the whale.

One day while sitting on the deck of the ship, the children watched the ship's crew harpoon a large porpoise and then struggle with it for several minutes before hoisting it aboard. Once it was aboard the boat they cut it up for the blubber; it was quite a spectacle to behold.

The majority of the crew had little to do with the emigrants and usually mistreated them. They appeared to Jane like a motley crew of misfits more suited to working with animals than with humans. There was one exception in the crew, and his name was Marcus, and he took quite a shine to the children. Marcus learned several tricks from ports around the world and was always willing to show them to Jane and the children. He was one of the most considerate individuals on the entire ship.

As the days passed, the family became familiar with several people on the vessel. Everyone had his or her own reason for leaving their homeland and coming to America, and the reasons were as numerous as the stars. Jane always enquired where their final destination was going to be, hoping to find someone headed to Michigan, but she never met anyone going in their direction. Many aboard the vessel had relatives already living in America, and they were going to settle near them. Several families were headed out west to seek the riches of the gold rush in California.

The voyage was not without its share of tragedy, unfortunately, and not everyone on the ship survived the voyage. On day twenty-one of the voyage, two elderly passengers who had been sick most of the trip died during the night. They were placed on cloth that was sewn into a sack. Before the sack was completely sewn shut, a rock was put inside it to weigh it down, and then the crew threw the bodies overboard.

On day twenty-six, a three-year-old girl that Eliza and Emma had played with on the ship died. She met the same fate as the two elderly people had five days earlier. Jane attempted to comfort the mother of the young girl but couldn't find the right words. The only thing she could do  was hold the young mother and cry with her. Jane thought to herself that losing a child must be one of the most difficult things a parent can experience, and she hoped that she would never have to endure the pain.

Day thirty-one saw the beginning of the worst storm of the entire voyage. Twenty-one-foot swells rocked and tossed the ship sadistically like it was a cork in a washing machine. The storm continued into the night and except for the occasional flash of lightning, the sky was pitch-black. Adding to the terror of the night was the deafening thunder, which made it difficult to sleep. The waves were so great that they came over the sides of the ship, and everything on the deck that wasn't fastened down was now floating in the ocean. Jane comforted the children as best she could, and they all slept huddled together that night.

Everyone was sleeping when at about two in the morning there was a loud crack that startled everyone, and then the screams began. The sleeping area was taking on water and the ship began to list to its port side.

The ship was now on its side and taking on water rapidly. Jane gathered as many of her children as she could in the darkness and screamed for the others to head to the exit. When they got to the exit they had no alternative but to jump into the ocean. Wreckage was floating all around the ship. Jane had four of the children with her and Eliza had two. As the ship took on more water, it began to break up and then vanished under the water, leaving a swirling area that sucked everything close to it under the water with it.

Jane, Eliza, and the remaining children managed to get to a large piece of wreckage of the ship floating near them. The women pushed the children to the center of the makeshift life raft and held on for dear life.

After what seemed an eternity, the storm subsided and the water calmed. Two children were missing: two-year-old Emma and six-year-old Mariah. Jane and the children started to scream the names of the missing children, but there was no reply. The storm had scattered the survivors far apart, and it was difficult to see in the darkness. Maryann was panic-stricken and began to rationalize with herself that the missing children were probably with other survivors and just too far away to hear their calls.

As the night progressed, the water became eerily still. The clouds overhead had passed, and they could see by the light of the moon. They could hear the cries of other survivors in the distance. Some cries were hysterical and frantic while others were the calm pleas of people trying to find loved ones.

More hours passed and it fell quiet. Jane, Eliza, and the children lay on the large piece of wood shaking from fear from their ordeal and the bitter cold.

Maryann saw it first: a silhouette of something very large moving toward their little island of safety. Then Eliza got a glimpse of its eye in the light of the moon. It was definitely moving deliberately into their path when Jane saw it and screamed for everyone to hold on.

The great white whale had found them and opened its mouth to swallow them, raft and all. The small craft with everyone aboard started to enter the whale's mouth, and as they did, drops of water from the roof of its mouth began to fall on them.

Maryann began to scream as she had never screamed before. She screamed a second time and said, "No. This can't be happening."

Jane shook Maryann and said, "Wake up!"

Maryann, who was wet from the drops of water that were falling on her from a leak in the ceiling above her, woke up. Jane asked her if she was all right and started to comfort her. Maryann, breathless from her nightmare, began to recount her horrible dream. It was so real to Maryann, but it was all a frightening dream.

By now all the children were awake, and when Maryann was done talking, Jane reassured the children that everything was going to be all right, and then she prayed for them. They all reclined and closed their eyes, but not everyone went to sleep.

Day thirty-two was a continuation of the day before, with unusually bad weather that brutally tossed the ship for most of the day. The *Isaac Wright* lost another passenger when a child was tragically swept overboard and lost.

Several uneventful days passed, and then one morning at sunrise someone spotted land and everyone tried to get their first glimpse of America. They first saw Long Island and Jersey Hill and then anchored at Staten Island, where they were quarantined. The entrance to New York Bay was captivating; the spotlessness was much different from Liverpool. Finally, thirty-seven days after they left Liverpool, on Thursday June 24, 1852, they reached New York Harbor.

The passengers would have to be cleared through quarantine before the ship could move into New York Harbor and they could disembark. Passengers were not offloaded directly to docks but onto smaller boats and tendered to shore. Before they were tendered to shore, they observed the spectacle on the docks: people scurrying everywhere hauling packages, venders selling goods—the children could hardly wait to get to shore.

When they got on shore, they would be beleaguered by scam artists and thieves who stole luggage, sold phony tickets to destinations west, and made life miserable for the immigrants. Jane and the children were approached several times with bogus offers before they could make their way to their boardinghouse. Twice they caught someone trying to make off with pieces of their luggage.

They were inundated with many distractions when they first reached land, but that did not detract from the actuality that they had survived the voyage and were in America. The air smelled fresher, the sky was bluer, the grass was greener, and everything appeared larger than back home. They screamed in unison, "Hello, America, we are here!"

Stagecoach and Train to a New Life

New York Harbor was quite a sight for the children. The first thing they noticed was the peculiar accent that most people had. The people spoke English but in a different way.

It was nice to be on land once more, but it took several days to get their land legs back. When they were sitting motionless, everything around them would start to sway as if they were still at sea, but their equilibrium adjusted to land and soon they were back to normal.

They spent a week and a half in New York City arranging transportation to Lynn, Michigan. Two women and eight children in New York City were like sheep among wolves, but they handled themselves well. Jane purchased a handgun while they were in the city and prayed she would never have to use it.

The city had a population of 500,000 people at that time, and because of the potato famine in Ireland, one-quarter of those New Yorkers were Irish. Crime was on the rise in the town, but thanks to the creation of the New York City Police Department seven years earlier, there were now twelve hundred police officers patrolling the streets. Before its creation, there were only fifty-one officers for the entire city.

The family made it to their boardinghouse and got unpacked. They had a large room that overlooked the street below. It only had three beds though, which meant that everyone took turns sleeping on the floor. The windows in the room were oversized and opened onto a balcony that they sat on to watch the sights of the city. Across the street was a saloon that thankfully closed at one in the morning, along with all its noise. Jane gathered everyone together, and they all took turns giving thanks to God for their safe trip there and asked for his continued help for the rest of the journey.

Jane and the children were all able to do odd jobs while in the city. They worked in the boardinghouse washing dishes, making beds, cleaning rooms, helping with meals, and running errands for the owner. The family earned enough extra money for Jane to procure some hardtack to eat on the trip, eating utensils, and a blue-backed speller for the children to read. Jane surprised the children with some hard candy; everyone savored each piece and tried to make it last as long as they could.

Before they left on the train and stagecoach, they tried to learn all they could about the cross-country journey to come. This poster was posted at several stagecoach and train stations:

#
Warning.

"Many stagecoach and train passengers are robbed while in

unfamiliar towns. Thieves are found near stage and train

depots, hotels, and taverns. Many even ride the stage and

train waiting their chance to rob prosperous-looking

passengers. Often boys who take your baggage to a hotel will

steal from you if you give them a chance. If you carry large

sums of money, buy a money belt. You might secure your

valuables in your luggage."

#

One rain-filled drizzling morning, Jane, Eliza, and the eight children boarded a train at Weehawken, New Jersey headed for Covington, Pennsylvania. There were thirty-two stops along the way at small and large towns. At each stop, there would be an exchange of passengers, and the children watched as travelers met loved ones waiting for them at the  stations. There were many hugs and countless tears as they greeted one another. The children often found themselves dreaming about the day they would reunite with their fathers.

At several stops, food could be purchased at the train station while the train refilled with water and re-supplied wood for its steam engine—wood was still the main fuel for the train but coal would take its place in three years. The cost of the train trip was three cents a mile, and the train traveled at a speed of four to ten miles per hour. The train pulled an entourage of passenger cars, baggage cars, house and platform-freight cars, and a caboose.

Train travel in 1852 was nothing like it is today. The passenger cars were narrow and passengers were packed into narrow seats with stiff backs. There were no adequate spark arresters on the engine or screens on the windows. At the end of a day's travel on the train, a passenger looked like he had spent a day in the blacksmith shop. Riding on the train was barely tolerable with the incessant jolting, rattling windows, dust, and lack of ventilation. It was so loud that conversation was attempted only when absolutely necessary. In 1852, train companies were beginning to divide train travel into classes depending on the luxury the traveler wanted and the money he was willing to pay. Third class was to be avoided at all costs. Third-class travel was reserved by regulation for pickpockets or other persons of dangerous character, as well as passengers affiliated with loathsome diseases, filthy and offensive clothing, or rude or indecent behavior.

The train traveled the New York and Pennsylvania border the first day and pulled into Binghamton, New York for their first layover of the trip. Binghamton was a larger town and had a nice boardinghouse that provided a room, supper, and breakfast for fifty cents.

Jane and Eliza were exhausted, and after supper and a good hot bath; everyone went to bed early that night. The children couldn't sleep and started to talk about what their new home might be like. They wondered if there would be children their age there and if they would have a school. They had learned about cowboys and Indians before embarking on the journey and wondered if they lived near their home. The children got so loud that they woke Jane. Jane reminded everyone that they would have to get up before the rooster crowed, and everyone quieted down and went to sleep.

They all got up at four a.m., had a hardy breakfast, and then walked to the train station as fast as they could because the train left at six a.m. exactly. The children watched the sunrise that morning from the train; it was breathtaking in the way it broke over the mountains, with each perfectly formed ray cutting through the heavy morning mist, making a kaleidoscope of colors. They strained to see the diverse array of wildlife that appeared in the countryside along the train route. About an hour into the trip, the train came to a screeching stop that threw everyone forward. The train had run into a herd of lumbering moose. After the tracks were cleared, they were on their way again.

At mid afternoon, the train stopped at a small town and everyone got off the train to have lunch. Jane and the children were standing in line at a large restaurant waiting their turn to be served. The aroma of the cooking food made everyone hungry and anxious to be served.

A nicely dressed older gentleman paid for his meal and was fumbling with money in his jacket pocket as he left. A five-dollar gold piece fell from the gentleman's pocket and rolled on the floor, stopping under a table in the corner of the room.

It was loud in the restaurant, and no one noticed the coin roll under the table. Six-year-old John watched the coin stop under the table, and when he saw that the older gentleman wasn't going to retrieve it, ran to the table, and crawled under it to get the coin. Without hesitation, he ran outside to the owner of the coin and told him he saw it drop from his jacket and onto the floor. He gave the coin to the man and the gentleman was so appreciative that he gave John a quarter as gratitude. John proudly paid for his lunch that afternoon and bought the rest of the family some candy with the money left over from lunch.

They pulled into Covington, Pennsylvania, their final train stop, just before sundown. Covington was a small village and the accommodations were less than desirable, but they made do with what they had. They found a restaurant that fed the entire crew of ten for a dollar, and that included apple pie. Now that they were fed, they had to rid their bodies of the black soot from the train engine that covered them head-to-toe. Their hotel did not have a bathtub, but two buildings down the street was a bathhouse that charged a nickel per person to get sparkly clean.

Feeling revived from the bath, they all ambled back to their hotel and got ready for bed. Jane had a surprise for everyone: earlier in the day at one of the train stops, she had purchased *The Cricket on the Hearth*, a novel by Charles Dickens. She read the first three chapters aloud, and then they all said their prayers and were fast asleep in minutes.

They spent the next day in Covington because the stagecoach only ran twice a week, and they were a day early for the next coach.

The day in Covington was relaxing in the morning; the family had a leisurely breakfast and then strolled around town window-shopping and getting some greatly needed exercise. After strolling for a while, Maryann became separated from the group. She was mesmerized by a dress she saw in one of the store windows and lingered at the store while everyone else moved on. Three young men saw her standing there, started to give her a hard time, and began making improper advances toward her. When Jane saw what was happening her feathers were ruffled and the children said they had never seen their mother become so irate. She gave the three young men such a verbal lashing they immediately backed off and were not seen for the rest of the time they stayed in Covington.

The children asked their mother what had gotten into her, and she calmly said, "That was pure love, children; love can be compared to a wild rose, attractive, serene, and lovely to smell but always willing to draw blood in its defense."

They spent the rest of the day washing clothes so they had something clean to wear when they finally got to Lynn. They purchased some lye soap from the general store, and the storekeeper's wife lent them her scrub board. They cleaned their clothes at a small creek just outside of town and brought them back to their room to dry, but they were still slightly damp the next morning when they packed and got ready to go.

They walked to the stage depot, and before they boarded the stagecoach headed for their new home, they were introduced to their driver. Charlie was a bearded weather-beaten man in his late forties who wore a dusty black hat and looked every part the cowboy. He had a handlebar mustache that he frequently stroked as he spoke. Charlie was a colorful man who was always spitting because of the chewing tobacco in his mouth. He always had some tall story to tell, and if you let him, he could talk you into a coma. For the most part his stories were interesting, and whether they were true or not, he told them with conviction.

The stage held only nine passengers, and their group had ten, so they had the entire stagecoach to themselves, with one of the children sitting on a lap. The fare for the stagecoach ranged in price from one to three cents a mile. The stagecoach had three seats inside, each of which accommodated three passengers. Those in the center isle and those with their backs to the horses faced one another and had to share leg space. It was cramped, hot, dusty, and bumpy inside the stagecoach. Jane and Eliza both wore scarves that helped cut down the dust they breathed from the road, and the children all wore bandannas. If it had not been for the beautiful landscape they were traveling through, it would have been pure misery.

Early pioneers with their heavy wagons carved out many stagecoach routes. In the rainy seasons the roads would get soupy, and it was easy for a stage to get stuck in the mud, so most stages carried a fence rail to pry the wheels out of mud holes. If the stage were stuck, passengers would have to walk with their luggage until they found dry land. Then they could re-board the stage and continue their trip. They were allowed only fifty pounds of luggage per person. The small children's bags were lightened and packed so they could drag them as far as they had to at each stop.

They traveled through the remainder of Pennsylvania, then Ohio and southern Michigan. The days of traveling were long, lasting from eight to twelve hours, and they would ride ten to fifteen miles between stations. While at a stagecoach station they were able to wash the dust from their bodies, stretch their legs, get something to eat, and buy food to take with them for the following day.

They would sleep under the stars most nights, but occasionally they slept in a barn, or in a boardinghouse if one was available and not too costly. Some overnight accommodations in the larger towns included a room and two meals (supper and breakfast) for fifty cents. Not all lodging was pleasant; some beds were dirty and full of vermin, so the floor was often a safer place to sleep.

Most meals cost twenty cents and included game entrees, seasonal vegetables, and delicious desserts. Stagecoach stations found in bigger towns even offered pastries and candy. At every station there was a blacksmith who could shoe a horse and repair the iron parts on the coach. There would also be horse tenders who unharnessed and harnessed the horses and took care of them. Inside the stagecoach were buffalo hides that the passengers wrapped up in when it was cold and sat on for comfort when it was not. The stagecoach carried not only passengers from station to station, it also carried the mail.

To help relieve some of the tedium of being cramped inside the coach, the children were allowed to ride topside. John Jr. was riding shotgun with Charlie one afternoon when Charlie started telling him stories about himself and Kit Carson. He and Kit Carson had hunted together in 1841 and 1842 in Colorado. He had been paid a dollar a day as a hunter for the U.S. government. While Charlie and Kit were together in Colorado, Kit met and married a Cheyenne woman named Making-Out-Road. The marriage only lasted a few months before she tossed his saddle out the door of their teepee, which was the accepted way for the Indians to get a divorce. Charlie and Kit went their separate ways when Kit was hired by John Fremont as a guide. John Fremont mapped and explored the Rockies. Charlie told John Jr. how Kit and he used to fight Indians and how the Indians used to scalp their enemies after battle. John Jr. was captivated but also frightened by Charlie's tales.

One memorable stop was in Pennsylvania on the national road at Mt. Washington Tavern. The house was built in 1816 on land that George Washington had once owned, and it was now a popular stagecoach stop. They made good time that day and pulled into the stop early. Charlie told everyone to sleep well and be ready to leave at the crack of dawn.

Charlie spent the night in the tavern and unfortunately got rather inebriated. It took several pitchers of cold water splashed on Charlie by the innkeeper and plenty of black coffee to get him moving the next morning. Thankfully, a seasoned team of horses was pulling the stagecoach that day because the family was on their own most of the morning as Charlie was quiescent until nine a.m., when he finally sobered up.

After their stop at Warren, Pennsylvania, they were on a stretch of road that followed Broken Arrow River. This stretch of road would take them to Erie, Pennsylvania, where they would catch a train to southern Michigan.

Broken Arrow was the most pristine portion of their trip from England so far. Most of the trail was uninhabited, and this is where they got their first glimpse of the American Indian.

It was mid-afternoon when they pulled into their first stop of the day to change horses and get something to eat. This stop was different because it was so quiet and no one greeted them as they pulled in. Charlie pulled the stagecoach up to the house and put on the brakes. He dismounted from the stagecoach and told everyone to stay put.

First he called out to see if anyone was there, but there was no reply. Charlie slowly walked into the house and found one of the men lying on the floor with an arrow in his back. It looked like there had been quite a scuffle in the house because everything was overturned. Charlie checked on the man lying on the floor; he was dead all right, and missing his scalp. Charlie walked out to the barn and found two more men missing their scalps lying on the ground. He searched the rest of the property but could not find the woman of the house or her three children. Charlie had made this stop before and knew the family well.

Charlie walked back to the stagecoach and called Jane from the coach. She got out, walked rapidly to him, and he informed her of what had happened. He told Jane not to let the children venture far from the coach. He got food from the house and asked Jane to feed the children and get water from the well. Charlie went to get a fresh team of horses from the barn, but all the horses had been stolen. He unharnessed the team, fed and watered them, and gave them a three-hour rest.

While the horses were resting, he dug three shallow graves for the three men and buried them. The children saw Charlie drag the bodies out back, and Jane was forced to explain to them what had happened. Charlie tried to downplay the whole incident, but he knew they were in trouble. He was hoping this was just a raiding party out to steal horses and prove their manhood. He knew that the Indians in the area had suffered the loss of women and children at the hands of a rival tribe. This was why the woman of the house and the children were not killed but stolen to replenish the tribe.

After resting the horses and doing what needed to be done, Charlie harnessed the horses again. Everyone boarded the stagecoach, and they were on their way. Jane rode shotgun with Charlie and carried a rifle, watching the road for any indication of trouble. They rode as far as they could until it got dark, then they made camp and had something to eat. Thank goodness they had hardtack with them because that was all they had to eat. The buffalo hide in the stagecoach kept them warm , and everyone except Charlie slept in the coach that night. Charlie slept under the coach and was ready for action if anything happened in the darkness.

No one slept soundly and as soon as it was daylight they were on their way again. Charlie was hoping to make the next stop by midmorning, but he was afraid to push the team of horses too hard, fearing that if he did, the horses might die.

Jane was riding shotgun with Charlie again, and as they rode, Charlie began to tell Jane some of his tales. He told her about the year he lived with Kit Carson, and how they used to hunt together. They were in the woods of Colorado hunting when six Indians ambushed them. Kit and Charlie killed three of the Indians and made the other three walk home bare-naked just to humiliate them. After Kit got a job with John Fremont, Charlie moved east and found employment driving the stagecoach.

They made it to the next stop by late afternoon, which was later than Charlie wanted, but he couldn't push the horses any faster than he had. This stop was just like the last—very quiet and no one greeted them as they drove up. Charlie dismounted from the stagecoach and again told everyone to stay where they were. He looked in the house and found two men lying dead on the floor. They had met the same fate as the others at the previous stop. Behind the house was the body of another man and a teenaged boy. Both had been scalped, and there were multiple arrows in their bodies. Charlie checked the corral and all the horses again had been taken. Without fresh horses Charlie knew they would have to spend the night and leave in the morning. Jane and Eliza helped Charlie bury the three men and boy and then made a meal while Charlie tended to the horses.

The night was going to be challenging because everyone was exhausted from trying to sleep in the stagecoach the night before. Soon the children were fast asleep. Charlie decided they should keep watch for any intruders. Jane, Eliza, Maryann, and Charlie took two-hour watches throughout the night. Charlie found another rifle in the house and added it to their small cache of weapons. They now had three rifles, Jane's pistol, and a Colt revolver (Walker model) that Charlie had purchased in 1850. Maryann and Eliza had never fired a weapon before so Charlie gave them a crash course on how to load and fire a gun. If they hadn't been in such dire straights, Charlie would have busted a gut laughing at the amusing way Eliza and Maryann held their rifles. Charlie decided it would be better for everyone to use the pistol for the night watch.

Maryann had the first watch and used Charlie's pocket watch to keep track of time. Maryann's watch was uneventful, and she woke Jane at eleven for her turn. Jane spent her two hours praying and watching, and before she knew it, it was one a.m. and time for Eliza to watch. Jane gave Eliza the pistol and timepiece, and then they talked briefly before Jane went to sleep.

There was a fire burning in the fireplace, and Eliza had just poured herself a cup of hot tea when the front door burst open and in ran two Indians. Eliza grabbed the pistol and shot the front Indian in the arm. Before she could get off a second shot, the other Indian threw his tomahawk at Eliza and hit her squarely in the chest. She fell to the floor in a heap, motionless. Three more Indians entered the house and jumped Charlie before he could discharge his rifle. Charlie wrestled with them as two other Indians stood guard over Jane and the children. Charlie put up a good fight, but he was outnumbered, and eventually he caught a tomahawk to the back of his head, ending his struggle permanently.

The Indians carried Jane and the children outside and set them on horses. They took Charlie's six horses from the stagecoach and, together with Jane and the children, rode off into the night. They rode for several hours until they got to the Indians' campground. They were shoved in a teepee with other white women and children who had been kidnapped from other farms and stagecoach stations in the area.

Everyone was dog-tired and eventually went to sleep. At sunrise they heard a commotion going on in the camp. It was the U.S. Cavalry, which had been dispatched to the area days earlier when reports of Indian trouble had been relayed to them. There were gunshots and people screaming outside their teepee, but Jane told the children to stay on the ground where they were. They didn't know what was going on, but it didn't sound good.

Everyone stayed still on the floor of their teepee until Jane stood up and opened the door flaps to look outside. As she opened the flaps a loud bang reverberated in the teepee and Jane fell backward into the tent and onto little John. He rolled her off him and discovered a bullet hole in her head. She was motionless, with blood flowing down her cheeks. John Jr. shook his mother and told her to get up, but she didn't move. He started crying and screaming for his mother when suddenly his body started to shake. They were small trembles at first and then larger shakes until his entire body was bouncing up and down. He opened his eyes and heard, "Wake up, John, it's okay. Momma's here." John Jr. was having the most horrific dream he had ever had—Charlie's tales were coming to life while he slept. After talking to his mother for a while he went back to sleep and slept for the rest of the night.

After two weeks of traveling on the stagecoach, they finally reached Lynn, Michigan. Their ordeal was over and the children were overjoyed when they finally reached their final stop and saw their fathers, whom they hadn't seen for over two years.

John Sr. was the first to see the stagecoach coming down the road, and he yelled to both Williams, "Here it comes."

The children were hanging out the windows of the coach as they drove up and spotted the men waving at them. They all started screaming, "It's Papa!" The stagecoach came to a stop and the children ran out and into their fathers' open arms as fast as they could.

Jane got a glimpse of John and started smiling from ear-to-ear. Then the emotions over all they had been through and the fact that it was now finally over hit her like an ocean, bringing waves of tears. She fell into John's arms. They kissed and hugged, and John said, "I have missed you so much. Never again will we ever be apart." They embraced for a long time, and the children, growing impatient, started to tug on John's pant leg, wanting their own hug and kiss.

John scarcely recognized the children; they had changed so much in the two years of separation. Emma was just a newborn when he left for America, and now she was walking. John Jr. looked like a young man even at the age of six; the journey had matured him beyond his years. They all got into a buckboard wagon and started to ride to their new home. Everyone had so many stories to share there wasn't one moment of silence all the way to the house.

After they arrived at their new home, they remembered the motto of their old home in Lincolnshire: *Perseverance Vincit*, "Perseverance Succeeds," and it had.

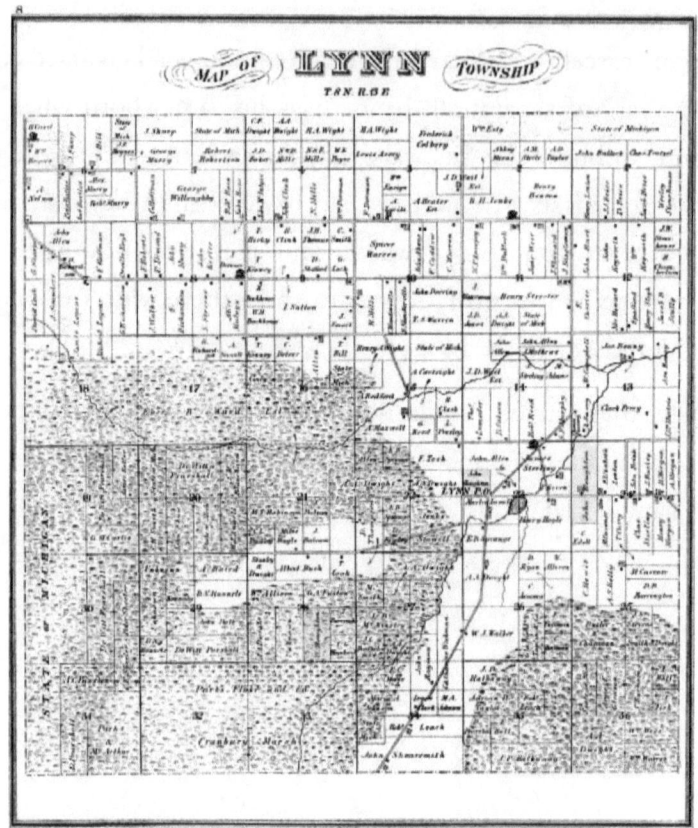

1876 map of Lynn Township. John Houghton's land, sections 23, 24, and 28.

Winter water wonderland

Lynn, Michigan

The Early Years
1852 -1860

With the help of Jane and Eliza, the men prepared a banquet for everyone to celebrate the arrival of the family. Elder William led the family in prayer, saying, "Blessed be the God and Father of our Lord Jesus Christ who has blessed us with all spiritual blessings in heavenly places through Christ and has given us eternal life through his son. Thank you, our Heavenly Father, for the safe arrival of everyone, and I ask Your blessing on our new home. Bless this family and their children's children with wisdom and may they love You and fear You all the days of their life. Amen and Amen."

The children could not remember the last time they had eaten so well. There was much work ahead of them and many trials, but for now it was a festive time and that was sufficient.

After eating and cleaning up, everyone went inside the cabin. Jane read the Bible by the light from the fireplace. She read one of her favorite passages in Matthew 6, in which Jesus said not to worry about the daily necessities of life, what you will eat, and what you will wear because your Heavenly Father knows you need these things and will provide them. You have to seek first the Kingdom of God and His righteousness and these things will be taken care of.

After Jane finished reading, everyone went to bed. It wasn't long before the children were dreaming about everything they had been through and what was in store for them in their new home, America.

The children quickly adjusted to the hard life of a pioneer family. Everyone had daily chores to do. John would gather eggs from the chickens, fetch water from the well, churn butter, and help feed all the farm animals: the family milking cow, Bessie and Harry the mules, of course, and the chickens and the horses. The chores would get increasingly harder for John as he got older because he was the oldest boy, but for now, the chores he had would do.

As the men continued to clear more land, the crops got bigger, the livestock became more plentiful, and the Houghton fare improved yearly. The children were expected to work on the farm, but time was set aside for schooling. There were no schools for the children to attend, so they were educated at home by John and Jane. The children learned how to read and write from reading the Bible, Dilworth's speller, and the blue-backed speller. They would borrow novels from neighbors, and it was always exciting when a new neighbor moved to the area because they might have a book the Houghtons had never read.

Only fifty-five other people lived in the township when the Houghtons arrived in Lynn, and only twenty-three million people lived in the entire United States. Milliard Fillmore was the thirteenth president and Michigan had been a state for only thirteen years. All three Houghton men would hold positions of leadership in the township at different times. The men narrowly missed the 1850 census, but they and their descendants have been in every Michigan census for 159 years.

News was slow in coming to the little community in 1852. That fall, after the women and children arrived, they learned through the *Port Huron Commercial*, the local newspaper, that Franklin Pierce had been elected the new president.

There was plenty to do on the farm and everyone kept busy, so busy that the years quickly flew by. William Jr. and his five children moved to their own farm during the fall, and William married a woman from Brown City. Eliza, Jane's younger sister, met a handsome French-Canadian blacksmith named Abraham (Abe) Savoy and got married. Abe could not read or write in English, so Eliza handled all the business for the family. They settled near the Houghtons and were a ubiquitous help in good and bad times. Although Jane tried for the rest of her life, she felt she could never repay her sister for her help with the children on their trip to America.

Here is a letter addressed to Elizabeth from William Sr. that was returned, stamped undeliverable. Postage was six cents.

Dear Elizabeth,   *July 23, 1853*

It has been some time since I last wrote you. Please excuse me but I have been busy clearing land and building a farm. I think you would be very proud of what we have accomplished here in such a short time with so limited resources. I have been living with John, Jane, and the children. Everyone is doing well and adapting to this new country. Our son William has remarried to a fine woman in another town not far from us. His children are all healthy and doing fine. I miss you a lot and think of you often. I understand and respect your decision not to come to America. How are you getting about in England? I hope all is well with you and Mary. I think you would love the wilderness here. There are so many different kinds of animals. I am learning something new nearly every day. John's children have adapted well to their new home and I am sure they like it here better than in England. They all miss you and send their love. There are new neighbors moving into the area and we now have a local store. Eliza, Jane's sister that helped her on her trip to America, was married three weeks ago, and lives not far from us. Her husband seems to be a nice man and they have been a big help to us on the farm. We now have a church building and there are nearly fifty people in attendance every Sunday. I hope to hear from you soon. I will always love you.

Love William

John and Jane had four more children after moving to America. They were:

1. Ellen (1854) – Lynn, Michigan

2. Jane (1856) – Lynn, Michigan

3. Richard Henry (November 24, 1857) – Lynn, Michigan

4. Elizabeth (1861 during the Civil War) – Lynn, Michigan

In 1854, Ellen was the first of John and Jane's American-born children. The family barely had time to get used to the new arrival when Jane (Janie) was born in 1856. Then the family blinked and along came Richard Henry in 1857; he was the second boy and sixth child. The house was getting too small for six children and three adults. Elder William, who lived with John and Jane, helped John build a new frame home.

They bought a three-blade walking gangplow in the spring that cut their plowing time in half, and they traded the mules plus twenty dollars for four Morgan horses. The Morgans were great utility horses because you could both plow a field with them and use them as saddle horses. Before the family bought the new plow, it would take about ninety hours of labor to produce a hundred bushels of corn from two-and-a-half acres using the harrow and planting by hand. It took 180 hours of labor to produce a hundred bushels of wheat from five acres.

The horses were valuable pieces of equipment on the farm, and if anything happened to them, the family's ability to make a living was severely hindered. At the beginning of planting season, the two bay Morgans were acting peculiar. They were resisting any work, and John noticed that they had been constipated but were now suffering from diarrhea. They knew the horses were eating something they should not. Young John watched them in the pasture and followed them as they grazed. He noticed the two horses that were having problems eating acorns and leaves from an oak tree, and he knew that oak leaves and acorns were bad for horses. What we know now, but John didn't know then, is that oak leaves and acorns contain tannic acid, which is poisonous to horses. John cut down the oak tree and cleaned the oak leaves and acorns from the pasture. He fed a mixture of bran mash to the horses to help flush their digestive tract of the poison and soon the horses were as good as new.

Times were tough and money was tight those first few years on the farm, but the Houghtons' door was always open to anyone in need. Everyone in their small community worked together to survive. When someone was in need of a barn, the community got together and had a barn raising. When someone got sick, everyone pitched in, helped plow fields, and made meals until the ill person got back on their feet. When someone got married or had a new child, everyone rejoiced together, and when someone died, they mourned together. They prayed together on Sunday and watched one another's back during the week.

Jane worked hard on the farm, cooking, cleaning, scrubbing, hauling water from the well to heat it on the stove, and keeping the fires going in the stove and in the fireplace most months of the year. She had to make all the family's clothes and take care of the children. She washed the family's clothes on a washboard at Mill Creek, at the  north end of their property. Washday was usually a family affair where everyone took part by scrubbing and rinsing the clothes and then taking the clothes back to the house to hang them on a clothesline to dry.

There were many peculiar animals in Michigan, and the family was slowing seeing them all. Early in the morning one chilly winter's day, John Jr. was walking to the north forty to do some hunting. He spotted a small animal dragging the carcass of an elk back into the woods. He was within a hundred yards of the creature when it stopped working on the elk and  gave John Jr. its undivided attention. At first it hissed and snarled, showing its sharp teeth, and then it charged him for about fifty feet and stopped. John Jr. could take a hint and started to retreat toward home. The creature went back to its kill and continued to drag it into the woods. Later John Jr. described the animal to his father, saying, "It sounded like the devil when it hissed and acted like it was a three-hundred-pound bear." He learned the creature was a wolverine, pound-for-pound one of the strongest animals on the earth.

In 1858, William campaigned for justice of the peace on the Republican ticket and was elected, and this began a long tradition of public service in the Lynn Township for the Houghtons. Armed with a copy of A *Treatise on the powers and duties of Justices of the Peace, in the state of Michigan, under chapter ninety-three of the revised statutes, with practical forms* by Anthony Tiffany, William was ready to uphold law and order in the township. It was easier to arrest a drunk than to say the title of his justice-of-the-peace manual.

The United States flag became one star larger with the addition of Minnesota to the union on May 11, 1858. The flag now had thirty-two stars, but this flag flew for only one year until Oregon became a state on February 14, 1859, bringing the count to thirty-three.

Thirty-two-Star Flag   **Thirty-three-Star Flag**

Page No. 63

SCHEDULE 1.—Free Inhabitants in Township Lynne in the County of St. Clair State of Michigan enumerated by me, on the 3 day of July 1860. Oliver Fedge Ass't Marshal

Post Office Lynne

1860 Federal Census. John and family at bottom of page. Houghton (Howton).

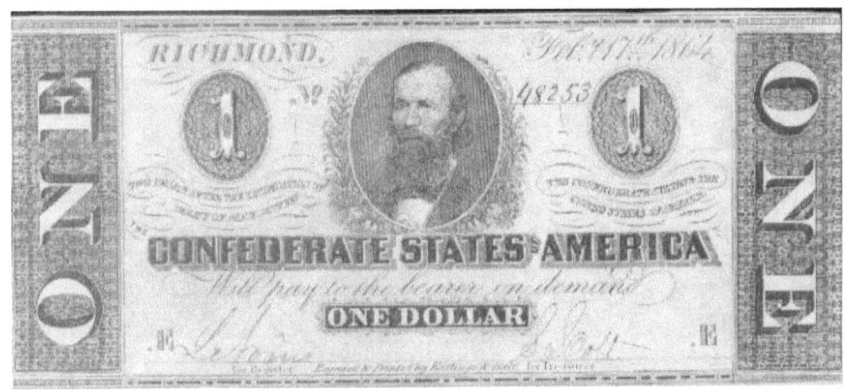

Becoming Americans

A War, a Death, and a Wedding
1860-1870

The family took part in the 1860 census, which revealed that over thirty-one million people now lived in America and 58% of those Americans worked on a farm. There were 751,110 people living in the state of Michigan, and the populace of Lynn Township was now 225 citizens, an increase of 170 people in ten years.

The census taker misspelled the Houghtons' last name during the first census in 1860. The Houghtons had a thick British accent and pronounced their last name "Howton." The census taker simply spelled it the way they were pronouncing it at the time. The ship's registry in 1852 from the *Isaac Wright* shows that Jane was spelling the name "Houghton." The 1870 census finally got it right.

Abraham Lincoln became the sixteenth president in 1860, and South Carolina was the first state to leave the Union.

John had a forty-acre parcel of land, a labyrinth of trees and vegetation, that he wanted to turn into a pasture. He was spending numerous hours each day felling trees on the property to make it functional. The majority of trees on the parcel were mammoth white pine. After cutting them down, John counted the rings in the trees' base that indicated their age, and the majority of them were nearly three hundred years old.

A byproduct of clearing the land was all the wood John now had. He used the trees to barter with the local merchant for goods at the store. The storeowner gave John a dollar and fifty cents' credit for each cord of wood he brought to the store. The wood from the north forty kept the family abounding with credit from the store for many years.

The Civil War began in 1861, and Elizabeth, the seventh and final child, was born just after the start of it. At the beginning of the war, the number of able-bodied men capable of service in Michigan was 110,000. By December 1862, more than 47,000 men had gone into battle, and by the end of the war Michigan had sent 90,747 men, or more than four-fifths of the number of men estimated as being able at the beginning of the war. One in six men from Michigan who served in the military during the Civil War would die, the sixth highest death rate among the Union states.

A close neighbor, Martin Lovell, whom the family had known since he first moved next to them at the age of seventeen, was one of the first in the area to enlist, at the age of twenty-three. He joined the Seventh Michigan Infantry Company A. In 1862, the war was going poorly for the Union Army and the Houghton family prayed nightly for the boys in blue. In the fall of that year, they learned from Martin

Lovell's family that Martin had survived the battle of Antietam and was promoted for meritorious conduct while in battle. That year, President Lincoln signed the Emancipation Proclamation, and it took effect in 1863.

In December, they read in the paper about the Indian uprising in Minnesota. The Sioux Indians, led by Chief Little Crow, killed over 400 settlers. General Sibley defeated the Sioux at Wood Lake and captured thirty-eight Indian prisoners. All thirty-eight were hanged in the largest mass execution in American history on December 26, 1862.

The way of life on the Houghton farm continued to improve every year, and they were getting to know everyone in their small neighborhood quite well. John was sociable and always had a kind word and smile for everyone he met, and in turn, he was well liked in the community.

In 1863, Ellen was nine and Janie seven, and they were inseparable. Janie's temperament and disposition made her almost a carbon copy of her mother. Ellen was easygoing and even though she was the older of the two, more often than not she would follow Janie's lead. Janie's thirst to know and do everything put Jane's parenting and teaching abilities to the test. Jane understood Janie the best of her children because they were so close in personality; Jane loved all her children but had an extra-special place in her heart for Janie.

The newspaper brought the good news of the Union victory at Gettysburg that summer and the bad news that their neighbor Martin Lovell had been wounded on July 3 during the battle. Later that year they became inspired when they read about Lincoln's Gettysburg address. By now their neighbors—Robert Leach of the First Michigan Engineers Company K; William Morgan, Fifth Michigan Cavalry Company E (the Fighting Michigan Wolverines, who defeated General Jeb Stewart at Gettysburg, commanded by Brigadier General George Armstrong

Custer); and Fred Hall, Third Infantry Company K—were all fighting in the war. John Jr. had been in America for only nine years when the war started, and was now turning sixteen years old. He and William Morgan of the Fifth Michigan Cavalry were close friends and often rode horses together.

The 1864 presidential election saw President Abraham Lincoln reelected. John's popularity in the township continued to grow, and as he had a reputation for faithfulness to public trusts, was known to use good judgment, and was noted for his qualities of leadership, it seemed only a matter of time before his name was put forward as a candidate for township supervisor. Ostensibly, his friends in the township did this in the summer of 1864. John was elected township supervisor on the Republican ticket that fall. This started the public-service phase of his life. People must have liked the way he ran the township because they reelected him every year until 1870. He was elected township treasurer in 1871 and stayed in the job until 1874; then he was township supervisor again from 1875 until 1877. He then served one term as constable and two terms as drain commissioner. The Republican Party appealed to John just as it did to other young men who hoped to get ahead; to him it held the promise of the American life. It stood for development, improvement, and advancement that removed class inconsistencies and seemed to give hope to everyone.

In May of 1864, John Jr. was asked by the Lovell family to travel to the train station at Capac to pick up their son Martin, who was returning from the war. John Jr. made the eight-mile drive with a buggy early in the morning, and by late afternoon, the train came chugging into the station. Many people got off the train, but John did not see Martin. John boarded the train and started going from car to car to find him. He then spotted a young man dressed in military uniform struggling with his luggage at the end of the car. John's mouth dropped open when the young man turned around and John realized he was Martin. Martin was on crutches and missing his right leg. John embraced Martin, welcomed him home, and then carried his luggage out to the buggy.

On their ride home, Martin told John about his experience in the Union Army. He talked about the enviable reputation the Seventh Michigan gained at Fredericksburg in December 1862. His company was the first to cross the Rappahannock River in pontoon boats, under fire from opposing sharpshooters, and they were able to drive the Confederate skirmishers from their cover.

At Gettysburg, his regiment was assigned a position at Cemetery Ridge on July 2 and held it until battle's end on July 3. Cemetery Ridge was the exact center of the Union Army line and where General Pickett would attack. Martin said that he saw the Michigan Cavalry brigade commanded by brigadier general George Armstrong Custer. The Michigan Cavalry Brigade consisted of four regiments of Michigan cavalrymen. Martin heard how General Custer personally led the Michigan Cavalry into battle shouting, ""Come you wolverines." During the battle on July 3, Martin was involved in hand-to-hand combat, when he was shot and bayoneted in the leg. Before he was carried back to the company hospital, where company surgeons Bolívar Barnum and Cyrus Bacon worked feverishly to save his life, he saw two of his closest friends shot to death. The bone in Martin's leg was so badly mangled that the only option was to amputate. Martin said that he was awake while they sawed his leg from his body because of a lack of anesthetic. The pain was so intense that he passed out twice until the leg dropped from his body onto the floor.

Martin's company played a key role in stopping Rebel efforts to break the center of the Union line in the third day of the battle. His company experienced twenty-one killed and forty-four wounded during the battle at Gettysburg. Martin spent nearly a year in Union hospitals recuperating from his surgery before being discharged from the army. John asked Martin what it was like in the hospital, and Martin hung his head and said, "The horrors are still too fresh to talk about."

In 1865, General Robert E. Lee surrendered his 27,000-man army to General Ulysses S. Grant at Appomattox Courthouse, Virginia, effectively and mercifully ending the four years of war. After four years of fighting and killing, nearly 10% of the U.S. population was obliterated.

The Civil War took its toll on the economy, but John continued to raise cattle, grain, and produce. Regardless of how much money people had, they still had to eat, and John was doing his part to feed them. John enlarged his cultivating fields and toiled extra-long hours raising bigger crops. They were even able to send their surplus to southern families in need of food.

All throughout 1865, the neighborhood boys that had left the area for the war were slowly returning home. Some were scarred physically and some emotionally but most were glad to be home. They all had stories to tell about the war and their travels through various states they had visited courtesy of the U.S. Army.

Janie

1866

The year 1866 started out as a banner year: the Houghtons had a large harvest, the barns were full, and the livestock was multiplying. John Jr. was now twenty, Eliza was eighteen, Emma sixteen, Ellen twelve, Janie ten, Richard nine, and Elizabeth was five. The children had adapted to the Michigan winter and enjoyed all the activities they could do in the snow.

They had many more neighbors now than when they first moved there, and once a month on Saturday night, they had a social at different neighbors' homes. The social would include a dance at someone's barn and games for the children. Twelve-year-old Ellen liked a boy from a farm two miles down the road. Leave it to outspoken Janie, who at ten was tall for her age, to do everything she could to get them together. Janie would tease Ellen, saying, "That boy might not be the pick of the litter, but at least he is nice." Ellen would chase Janie around the barn but couldn't catch her.

In 1866, it was not appropriate to ask a boy to dance, so at the socials Janie would ask the boys to dance with her sister Ellen. Ellen pretended to be embarrassed when Janie asked a boy to dance with her but inside she was thankful.

The two girls talked to each other about meeting the boy they would one day marry. Ellen's Mister Right had to be tall and handsome with lots of money and want a big family. Janie didn't want to get married for a long time yet, so her Mister Right had to be someone from far, far away. Ellen made Janie give her word that when she got married Janie would be her maid of honor. They were content that winter and all was right with the world.

Spring weather came early that year but not early enough for the children, who were suffering from cabin fever; now with the warmer weather they were able to do more things outdoors. They had the usual chores to do, but spring meant getting ready for summer planting. They had fifty head of cattle now and the cattle would soon begin to calve. It cost about $3.50 to raise a beef cow to maturity, and they could get $30 a head. They gave extra attention to all the heifers on the farm as it got closer for them to calve.

All the children had a favorite animal on the farm to which they gave extra attention and care. Janie was attached to a cow she named Lucie. Lucie was born when Janie was five, and Janie fell in love with her when she was a calf. This spring Lucie was pregnant and about to calve herself. Lucie was extraordinarily large and John thought she might be expecting twins.

As it got closer to the time for Lucie to have her calves, Janie started sleeping in the barn so she could be present to get her father to help birth the twins. The night finally came. Janie knew that Lucie was close to birthing from the telltale signs Janie had seen throughout the day. Lucie began to bellow and her water broke, and Janie ran to the house to get her father. John delivered the first calf without a hitch, and it was on its feet soon after delivery. The second calf was breach, and no matter how hard John struggled to get the calf out, he could not. Lucie and the second calf died in the early morning. Janie could hardly see through the tears as she kissed her friend good-bye.

She scarcely had time to grieve for Lucie because she heard a noise behind her and turned around to find the new calf lying in the straw. She crawled over to it, began to check it out, and discovered that it was a girl. Therefore, the only logical thing to do was to name her Lucie. Janie was now her surrogate mother, and a good mother she was. 'Little Lucie', as Janie called her, was like an oversized puppy. The calf was allowed to roam freely and followed Janie wherever she went.

After planting season came summer, a more relaxed time for everyone. After a hard day's work everyone would meet at Mill Creek to cool off. They spent many hours fishing there, and this is where they caught their first walleye. The girls liked to catch fish but didn't like to bait the hook with a worm. The boys were happy to do this because that meant more fish to eat. The boys liked to eat the fish so much that the first catch was usually  cleaned immediately, put on a stick, and cooked over a small fire next to the river. They would eat it while they angled for more.

Mill Creek was like their own fish market, teeming with walleye, perch, bass, bluegill, trout, and catfish. The boys spent many hours of their leisure time making withdrawals from the river and deposits to their stomachs.

Mill Creek was deep enough and large enough for the children to ride the horses bareback to the creek and go swimming with them. The horses would tread into the water until the water was over their backs, and then the children would float off the back of the horse and grab its tail. The horse would then pull them around the water with its tail.

There were several wild cherry trees on the farm, and the children spent many hours picking cherries for their mother. Jane had a prize-winning recipe for cherry pie, and the children knew that if they collected enough cherries they could help her make the delicious treat. They resisted eating the cherries as they picked them, but one out of ten usually made it to their stomachs before it became a pie.

One day that summer Janie complained to her mother that she did not feel well. Janie may have been only ten, but her mother often said that she was wise beyond her years. Her father had the doctor visit the house to check on her. The doctor didn't know the exact reason for her illness; he knew only that something was very wrong because she was growing weaker every day and had trouble eating.

Every window in the house was open that summer, but it still got sultry inside. At night, Janie's mother would take her outside where it was cooler, and they would lie on the ground and look up at the sky and just talk. They talked about everything and nothing. One night Jane asked her daughter if she was afraid to die. Janie said, "When I look at the stars I recognize there has to be more to life than just living and dying. I am not afraid of dying because you and Daddy have explained to me about heaven and Jesus. The only thing I'm anxious about is not having enough time to figure out my place in this world before I have to leave it." Janie was always brave and courageous; she might have had an illness, but the illness did not have her. Janie possessed fortitude, a firmness of spirit, a steadiness of will in doing good despite all obstacles, and a lack of fear in the face of major pain.

Jane would become emotional and cry when Janie talked so maturely. Jane would try to hide the tears from her daughter, but Janie always knew when her mother was crying. Janie would wipe the tears from her mother's eyes and reassure her that everything was going to be all right. At times like that Jane wondered who the grown-up was, Janie or her.

When they were outside, little Lucie would lie next to Janie like a dog. Janie would pet her and Lucie would lick her with her long, coarse tongue.

Janie's illness was tough on everyone, but exceptionally hard on Ellen; her best friend in the entire world could not participate in any summer activities. Ellen promised Janie she would be her best friend until the end of time, and they would be together forever. Janie always seemed comforted when Ellen held her hand and sang to her. Her favorite song was *Footsteps of Angels* by Henry Wadsworth Longfellow. The poem had been made into a song and the third verse was her favorite:

And with slow and noiseless footsteps

Comes that messenger divine,

That the vacant chair beside me,

Lays her gentle hand in mine.

And she sits and gazes at me

With those deep and tender eyes,

Like the stars, so still and saint-like

Looking downward from the skies.

Like the stars so still and saint-like

Looking downward from the skies.

Janie would close her eyes when Ellen sang and say she could see the angels. Ellen often wondered if she was in the company of an angel when she was with Janie.

Ellen stayed close to Janie all that summer and cared for her as if she were her child. It got difficult for Janie to walk, so Ellen and John Jr. made a cart and lined it with blankets and pillows. Ellen would help Janie get in the cart, and she would pull her around the farm.

Janie's favorite place on the entire farm during the summer was under the shade of a large oak tree near Mill Creek. Janie and Ellen would throw twigs into the water and watch them float down the river. Some days Ellen would pack a lunch and they would sit next to the river, enjoy the symphony of nature, and put all the cares of the world out of their minds.

The summer was now nearly over and Janie was growing weaker every day. Ellen had to carry Janie to the cart for their daily ride around the farm. They would always end up at Mill Creek and sit for as long as Janie could tolerate being outside. Even with the summer heat, she was having trouble staying warm without being covered. She had a favorite blanket that Ellen always brought along to cover her. It was quite a sight when Ellen pulled Janie around with the cart because little Lucie would always tag along.

Ellen stayed at Janie's side day and night and made sure Janie had whatever she wanted. Ellen, sooner than the others, noticed the fast progression of Janie's illness. Ellen was now feeding Janie, and when she wouldn't eat, Ellen would become angry and make her take a bite of food. Janie's breathing was now labored, even at rest, but she still insisted on her daily cart ride around the farm.

Janie was finding it difficult to speak, but when she did speak, she always talked about her heavenly home. She described her heavenly home as this beautiful, fantastic place where she could run and play with the other children; a place where pain was nonexistent and everyone was always happy. It was a home where everything was perfect, even her body, and the views from her new palace were spectacular. When she spoke of heaven, her face had an angelic radiance, and Ellen would become mesmerized by her words.

One morning Janie could not open her eyes or respond to the desperate pleas of her mother to talk to her. Ellen was frantic and pleaded with God to wake her sister up and make her well again, but it was to no avail, and Janie never regained consciousness. Her breathing became labored, then shallow, and then her body became still. She died that morning. John and the rest of the family were on the front porch, and when they heard the uncontrollable sobbing from Jane and Ellen, they knew the worst had come.

Jane could not understand why this had happened. Parents should not bury their children; children should bury their parents. She couldn't make sense of Janie's death. How could this benefit anyone? Jane was angry and she let God know it. She let everyone know that she needed some time alone and went off by herself to just talk to God. After a few hours of heated conversation, she cried herself to sleep. She awoke with a sense of peace—not the peace that the world can understand, but "that peace that surpasses all understanding", a peace that comes only from having a personal relationship with a personal God.

That doesn't imply that Jane was not human because Janie's death was a sensitive wound that subjected her to bouts of melancholy and depression. The wound would heal with time but many say a part of Jane died with her daughter that summer.

Ellen was devastated by the death of her sister and for the rest of her life could never talk about her without lament; Janie was supposed to be her maid of honor but never got the chance.

The family had a funeral for Janie at their home because there were no funeral homes in the area at that time. Embalming cost seven dollars in 1866, but there were no embalmers to perform the duty. It wasn't until 1868 that states were required to keep a registry of deaths, and consequently there is no formal record of Janie's death.

Before the coffin was closed and Janie's body was taken to her gravesite, Ellen covered her with her favorite blanket; she could not stand the thought of her sister getting cold. They carried Janie's coffin out to the wagon and drove to her gravesite. As they made their way to bury her, little Lucie tagged along behind the wagon, bellowing as if she knew who was in the coffin.

The family's pastor gave a eulogy, and then every family member had a word of farewell as they tossed a handful of soil onto the wooden coffin. Five-year-old Elizabeth did not understand death, and earlier in the day when the coffin was open, she asked her father why Janie was sleeping in the box. When Elizabeth's turn came to say her farewell, she said in her innocence, "See you when you wake up, Janie." She then tossed her handful of soil onto the coffin, dusted her hands together, and smiled at her mother.

Jane's turn came and she struggled to keep her emotions in check because what she had to say was extremely important. She spoke about her time alone with God shortly after Janie's death and how she was so angry with Him. After she gave God a piece of her mind, God began to speak to her softly and reassuringly, and these thoughts are what gave her peace. Jane said, "The thing that Janie and I had the most in common is the very thing that assures me the most of her well-being, and that was our faith in Jesus Christ. Because of the resurrection of Jesus Christ, the scariness, the horror, and loneliness of death melts away, and I know beyond a shadow of doubt I will someday see her again. After that, I knew that life must and will go on." As Jane tossed her handful of soil onto the coffin, she said in a determined voice, "I will see you in heaven. I love you, Janie."

Everyone dealt with Janie's death in their own way. John Jr. dealt with it by staying busy. He and William Sr. dug the hole for Janie's coffin and lined it with boards. They buried her under an oak tree near Mill Creek, her favorite place on the property.

Janie's death made everyone old enough to understand a stronger person. While Jane was healing from the loss of her daughter, she remembered the young mother on the ship *Isaac Wright* who lost her three-year-old daughter. Jane tried to comfort her but could not find the words and could only hold her and cry with her. Now Jane and the family had dealt with the anguish of losing someone so young and so close to them and could now see the light on the other side. This equipped them to reassure others, for with the comfort they had received they could now comfort others. Jane realized that God had His hand on every trial and tribulation they were faced with, and He would allow the family to become stronger through them. His undying love and compassion pulled them through the heartbreak, and the weaker they became the stronger He grew inside them.

Little Lucie noticed that Janie wasn't around any longer. She seemed lost and would wander aimlessly around the property looking for her surrogate mother. Soon after Janie's death little Lucie went missing, and John Jr. found her half-eaten carcass down by the river.

The next day Jake came into the family's life and brought a ray of happiness that the family sorely needed. He would remain with them for the next twelve years. Jake was a stray dog of mixed breed and less than a year old; he was brown with black and white spots. He had the happiest eyes and most affectionate disposition. He would become a loyal family friend and trustworthy watchdog.

U.S.

ADD TIME NEWS

INSIDE: Main | The Page | Politics | Swampland | Real Clear Politics | White House Photo Bl

Teaching Ling a Thing

Friday, Aug. 25, 1967

Print   Email   Share   Reprints   Related

One of the sharpest corporate skirmishes in memory swirled around Milwaukee last week, as Allis-Chalmers Manufacturing Co. found itself under heavy assault. The battle was joined by James Joseph Ling, 44, chairman of Dallas-based Ling-Temco-Vought, who during a nine-day fight for control of the company had eventually made a tender offer valued at $560 million—one of the biggest ever. But by week's end, staid Allis-Chalmers, which is the area's biggest employer, had delivered L-T-V its first defeat—however temporary—in Ling's long takeover history.

Looming Large. Ling's campaign naturally provoked nationwide fascination. Starting with a $3,000 stake in 1946, he had wired together a series of dazzling acquisitions to build a conglomerate that topped $468 million in sales last year. And this year "the Ling Dynasty," as L-T-V is sometimes called, has loomed even larger. In March a surprise Ling tender offer hauled Chicago's Wilson & Co. into the fold. Early this month, Ling announced a plan to take over Greatamerica Corp., the Dallas-based bank, insurance and airline (Braniff) combine controlled by his longtime ally, Troy Post. If Ling could take Allis-Chalmers in hand L-T-V bid fair to quickly become a $3 billion company.

Allis-Chalmers has 38,000 employees, runs 20 plants in the U.S. and Canada, is the third biggest U.S. maker of electrical and construction equipment and fourth in farm machinery. Under Chairman Robert Stevenson, 60, a minister's son who started off as an Allis-Chalmers tractor salesman in 1933, profits have more than quadrupled since 1961 to last year's $26 million, on record sales of $857 million. For all that, the company recently ran into trouble. The general slump in construction, rising production costs and a sticky three-month strike at two plants combined to plunge first-half earnings down by 50% compared with the same period last year.

To Ling, that seemed to ripen a prospect he had been watching for more than three years. In the military argot current at his Dallas headquarters, Allis-

Time magazine 1968, Robert S. Stevenson, chairman Allis-Chalmers.

Walter and Robert S. Stevenson

1867 1908-1983

The summer of 1866 stretched everyone's faith to the limit. Thankfully, Jane had a lot to do later that fall that helped change the mood in the house and take Janie's death off her mind. She had to help plan the first wedding of the Houghton children in America: Eliza, their second child, married Steven Stevenson, who was from Maple Valley, Michigan. She was eighteen, he was twenty-four, and they were married in Brockway, Michigan on Sept 10, 1866 by their minister Donald Brown.

The year after their wedding, they had a boy named Walter, born on July 21, 1867. Shortly after Walter's birth, Steven became ill, left the family, and was never heard from again. Eliza and Walter lived with John and Jane for the next seven years.

Eliza married Daniel Cartwright in 1874 and moved to Gilford, Michigan. Walter continued to live with John and Jane, and they raised and educated him as if he were their own child. They knew from a young age that Walter had an extraordinary call in his life. He grew up to be an ordained Presbyterian minister and moved to Wenatchee, Washington.

Walter married Della, and they had a son named Robert S. Stevenson, born November 10, 1908. Robert married Savannah and had a daughter, Ramona, born 1930.

Robert S. Stevenson became the president of Allis-Chalmers Company in Milwaukee, Wisconsin from 1955 to 1968. Robert joined the company in 1933 as a sales assistant and through hard work and pure genius worked his way to the top and became president of the company.

He retired in 1968, but during his tenure as CEO, profits quadrupled. In 1968, the company was worth over 586 million dollars with over 38,000 employees.

Robert remembers stories his father Walter would tell from the pulpit about his Grandmother and Grandfather Houghton and how God used them to help shape him into the person he became. He admired their work ethic, selflessness, duty to community, and love for their family. Robert moved to Farmington Hills, Michigan after he retired and died there on March 18, 1983.

1868

In 1868, Ulysses S. Grant became the eighteenth president of the United States and John was reelected township supervisor. Farming equipment was improving every year, and they had to keep updating their equipment to stay competitive. They bought a new sulky plow and four more Morgan horses, which made John Jr.'s life a little easier. John Jr. was now twenty-two years old and doing most of the plowing on the farm. The plow cost seventeen dollars but was worth every penny because of the time it saved. They were using 120 acres for planting crops and forty acres for pasture. It cost them about four cents to produce a bushel of corn, and they earned on average $1.31 for a fifty-six-pound bushel. They added a pair of mules named Polly and Jackie to the plowing duty as well. Polly and Jackie were a matched pair and so easy to drive that Richard, now eleven, could easily handle them. Now it was possible to plow twice as much as before.

That fall trusty old Jake was missing for three days, then one night he came limping back to the farm, swollen, bleeding, and full of porcupine needles. It seems that Jake had lost his first and last fight with a porcupine. John Jr. and the girls spent the night pulling needles out of

Jake and bathing him. He quickly recovered and was soon his old self again.

On August 10, 1868, war parties of Cheyenne, Arapaho, Kiowa, Comanche, Lakota, and Pawnee raided white settlements in Kansas, Texas, and Colorado. The raid in Kansas resulted in fifteen white settlers killed and many wounded, with women being raped and taken captive. General Sheridan sent in the Seventh Cavalry, led by George Armstrong Custer, to apprehend the guilty. This led to the battle of Washita River near Cheyenne, Wyoming, where approximately fifty Indians and twenty-one soldiers were killed. Twenty of the slain soldiers were from a small detachment led by Major Joel Elliot. Major Elliot separated from the main company in pursuit of escaping Indians without the permission of General Custer. Elliot and his men ran into a much larger group of Indians and were overwhelmed in a single rush that annihilated them all.

Richard Henry was enthralled by the battle and read all he could about it in the paper. Richard was so captivated by the West and his hero General Custer that he asked his parents permission to join the Seventh Cavalry. Richard was eleven at the time and his parents told him to wait until he was eighteen before asking again. They hoped that the fascination would pass with time.

Later that year William Sr., now seventy-six, filed naturalization papers to become an official American. During the swearing-in procedure, William had to raise his right hand and disavow his allegiance to the Queen of England. He was so proud of that day that he had his picture taken to commemorate the event.

17H

DECLARATION OF INTENTION.

Printed and sold by Creighton, Hepburn, & Co., Detroit, Mich.

COPY.

STATE OF MICHIGAN, } SS.
COUNTY OF *St. Clair* } The *Circuit Court for said County, to-wit*:

I *William Houghton*

solemnly swear that it is bona fide my Intention to become a **Citizen of the United States,** and to **RENOUNCE FOREVER,** all Allegiance and Fidelity to each and every Foreign Prince, Potentate, State or Sovereignty whatsoever, and particularly the *Queen of Great Britain* whom I have been a subject.

W. E. Houghton

Sworn to and subscribed before me, at *Muzzy* this *22* day of *February* A. D. 186*8* [SIGNED.]

Ezra Hagen Dept. Clerk

William Houghton naturalization papers, 1868.

William Houghton, 1868.

1870 Federal Census. John and family near the bottom of document. Name
spelled 'Houghton'.

The Changing Family

1870-1880

In 1870, the family took part in their second federal census. There were now over thirty-eight million people living in America and 53% of those Americans were farmers. Lynn had grown to 539 people and had a post office, several stores, shops, a hotel, and even a cheese factory. The closest shipping was on the Huron and Lake Michigan railroad,

found eight miles south of Lynn at Capac. Also in 1870, Georgia would be the last former confederate state readmitted to the Union.

John was building a herd of cattle in 1871 and was in need of a prize bull around which to build the herd. He learned of a herd at Port Sanilac, Michigan that was two days' horseback ride from his farm. They were selling a trophy bull that John wanted to buy.

Early on the Friday morning of October 6, John and John Jr. saddled their horses, packed their saddlebags and headed out to buy a bull. Both men holstered a sidearm and carried a rifle for the trip. As they rode northeast to Port Sanilac, they talked about the various items on the farm that needed mending. John Sr. was concerned about a stretch of fence on the north forty that needed repair, two horses that needed new shoes, and the barn roof, which needed some attention.

It was quiet that morning as they rode, except for the chirping of the birds and *clip-clop* of the horses, there was not another sound. A lot of wildlife was on the move that morning. They saw wild turkey and a lynx, and if they had been on their way home, they would have shot one of the elk they saw. Overhead they could see turkey buzzards circling something that had died or was dying, and when they got to where they were, they discovered several dead deer. They looked like they had been shot and the carcasses left to rot. The turkey buzzards were waiting their turn to eat because foxes had beaten them to the deer. At midday, the men stopped at a river, watered the horses, and let them eat as they themselves ate and filled their canteens from the river.

After they ate, they continued on their way, talking as they went. This was the first time in quite a while that the two men had been alone and had a chance to talk. John Jr. told his father that he wanted to ask a girl from church on a date. John Sr. asked the young woman's name and John Jr. said, "Carrie Wickham." John Sr. liked the Wickham family and approved of his son's choice.

They rode until it got dark and made camp for the night just past Lexington, Michigan. They rose at sunrise, had breakfast, and were on their way again. The air was crisp and the view was spectacular, with all the multicolored leaves on the trees. They rode along Lake Huron and occasionally got glimpses of the lake from the road. They were thankful they hadn't been rained on during the night. Michigan and all the Midwest were in the midst of a severe drought and though the men would be happy for some much-needed rain, they hoped it could wait until they got home.

Day two was pleasant and they reached their destination by mid-afternoon. They picked out a bull they liked and began to negotiate a price for him. They settled on a price, bought him, and started on their way home again.

They were making good time, considering having to contend with the bull. When it got dark, they stopped and camped out again. During the night, they could smell smoke from a big fire, and by morning they could see the flames. They had to stay next to the lake and at one point had to hold up until the fire went by and it was safe to travel again. The fire cost them an extra day's travel, but they finally made it home and were relieved to see that the flames had missed their area and everyone was safe.

That forest fire claimed over two hundred Michiganders' lives and burned over 1.2 million acres of land in the thumb area. The same drought affected Chicago, and on the same day as the Michigan fire, October 8, 1871, Chicago had its own legendary fire, known as the Great Chicago Fire.

Shortly after their trip for the bull, John Jr. started courting the young woman he had met at church, Caroline (Carrie) Wickham. Caroline had caught his eye right away, but it took a while for her to catch his heart. Caroline and her parents had moved to Lynn from Canada in 1867 when she was twelve years old. She had to do some growing, but after she did John fell in love with her. He could hardly wait for Saturday nights because he would hitch up the surrey and drive over to Caroline's parents' house for supper. When they were done eating, they would sit on the front porch with the family and talk.

It took several months of courtship before John could work up the courage to ask Caroline to marry him, but the night finally came. John was shined up like a brand-new silver dollar that night, wearing his Sunday-best clothes. After supper, Caroline and John went for a walk, and Caroline could sense something wasn't right because John was so nervous. When they walked back to the front porch, Caroline sat on the swing and John knelt in front of her. His palms were sweating and his heart was beating so fast he thought it might explode. He told Caroline that he loved her, and he could not imagine life without her. Then he asked Caroline if she would be his wife. She began to cry and said, "Yes, I will."

John had asked her father's permission to marry her several days prior, he had said "yes" but didn't tell anyone. Caroline's family were all sitting inside the house at the front door listening, and when Caroline said yes, they all burst out onto the porch and showered both of them with hugs and kisses.

John Jr. and Caroline became one on July 3, 1872. There was a large celebration after the wedding and all the community was invited to attend. John Jr. and Caroline postponed their honeymoon for a month to get settled on their new farm but left for Niagara Falls, Canada on August 17, 1872.

This was John and Caroline's first trip together. They spent two weeks in Niagara Falls enjoying the sights. They visited the falls, of course, and learned that 20% of the world's fresh water lies in the Great Lakes and uses the falls as its outlet.

While they were there, they were treated to a real buffalo hunt staged by Sidney Barnett. Barnett went to the Indian Territory out West and hired several Soc and Fox Indians and Mexican cowboys to perform in the show. He purchased buffalo for the hunt, and while he was in Kansas City, he met Wild Bill Hickok, one of the most daring and striking scouts of the West, and hired him to go east and manage the Niagara Falls Buffalo Hunt.

Wild Bill was the master of ceremonies and the performance was on two days, August 28 and 29. John and Caroline attended the performance on the 28th. The show was action-packed and something they would remember for the rest of their lives.

Being originally from Canada, Caroline still had relatives living there. They visited her relatives and after two weeks of relaxing returned to Lynn, Michigan to start their life together.

Later that year President Grant was re-elected president by a landslide and passed the Amnesty Act that restored all civil rights to southern citizens. John was elected to his second term as township treasurer.

In 1873, a fellow Michigander, General George Armstrong Custer, and the Seventh Cavalry engaged the Sioux Indians for the first time during the Indian Wars. Also in the same year, a Wall Street crash would send America into a financial depression for five years.

Great-Grandfather John Jr.

1872-1880

Great-Grandfather John Houghton came to America with his mother Jane when he was just six years old. John worked hard on his father's farm to make it the best in southern Michigan. His father and mother, who could both read and write, educated John. At the age of twenty-six, on July 3, 1872, John married Caroline Wickham, at Lynn. Caroline, seventeen, born on January 8, 1855 in Sombra, Canada, was the daughter of John Wickham, born 1819 in Canada, and Catharine, born 1831, also in Canada.

John moved from his parent's home after the wedding and started his own farm and family in Lynn.

John Jr. and Caroline had six children. They were:

1. Andrew, born August 13, 1873 in Lynn. (He lived two months and twenty-five days.)

2. Catherine Jane, (Katie) born September 11, 1874 in Lynn.

3. Ruby E., born December 17, 1876 in Lynn.

4. Anna Elizabeth, (Bessie) born December 22 1879 in Lynn.

5. Maud Caroline, born August 4, 1884 in Mecosta.

6. Grandfather John III Donald, born January 5, 1893 in Mt. Pleasant.

In August of 1873 their first child, Andrew, was born. He had brown hair and Caroline said he looked just like his father. John Jr. was as proud as a peacock and put all his hopes and dreams into his son, who he hoped would someday work with him on the farm. Two months and twenty-five days later, Andrew died from pneumonia. Caroline was inconsolable and spent a month holed up in her bedroom. John Jr. asked his mother and father to come over to the house and talk to Caroline. They did and they talked and prayed until the wee hours of the morning. Caroline had a breakthrough and from then on John Jr. and Caroline kept themselves busy on their new farm, which helped to ease the pain of losing their son.

Life was hectic on the farm that next year after the loss of Andrew, and before they knew it, along came Caroline Jane, born Sept 11, 1874. She was named after her mother and grandmother. John Jr. could scarcely wait for the day he could take her to church and show her to all his neighbors. John Jr. was so proud of her he nearly burst a button on his shirt.

John was making major improvements on the farm year after year even though times were tough, due in part to the depression the country was going through. They did not have many possessions, but they always had food on the table, and they had one another. Whenever anyone was hungry, John would quote Psalm 37-3: "Trust in the Lord and do good. So you will live in the land and will be fed."

Later that year, Ellen, John Jr.'s younger sister, married Jonathan Steinhoff and there was a big celebration and dance at the Millers' barn. Before Ellen walked down the aisle at the church, she thought about her younger sister, Janie. Ellen remembered the pact she had made with her sister when she was a young girl. A tear started to come to her eye as she remembered how they played together as young girls and talked about the day Ellen would marry. The tears began to freely flow as she remembered the day Janie died. However, Ellen dried her eyes and put on a false face of bravado—her wedding was about to start, and she had to be strong. Later that night at the wedding celebration, Ellen gave a special tribute to Janie, who was supposed to be her maid of honor but had been called home by heaven before she got the opportunity.

In 1876, they read in the paper about Custer's last stand at Little Bighorn. Custer's death hit Richard Henry rather hard. Richard was eighteen and getting ready to leave home to join his childhood champion. The man he had idolized for so long, the boy general and Civil War hero, was now dead. Richard spent the rest of the summer trying to decide what he was going to do with his life, and in the end he decided to work with his father, the only other man who, in his eyes, measured up to Custer.

The death of Custer could not have come at a worse time because the country was gearing up for America's one-hundredth birthday celebration. On July 4, 1876, the community of Lynn had an enormous birthday celebration for America. Everyone in the community flew flags, and all the shops were decorated with banners. There was a large community picnic and games for children of all ages.

It was customary to have an invited guest or someone of importance in the community give a speech before the picnic began. This year John Sr. was chosen because of his many years of service to the community. John spoke about his life as an American, how he and his family had traveled from England to Lynn, Michigan, and how the community had changed over the past twenty-six years since he had moved there. "When I arrived here with my father and brother," he said, "there were only fifty-five other people in the township, and now there are nearly 600. We have a post office, hotel, and shops, and the area is much more civilized now. We have the freedom to express ourselves and go wherever we please. God has blessed my family and he has blessed America. It is truly a pleasure to live here and serve my neighbors; you are a great group of people. May God always bless America, the land that I love."

That night they enjoyed a fireworks display that was so colossal and spectacular it was talked about for many years afterward. America was now a hundred years old, and William Sr. prayed that she would never get too old to carry the torch of freedom.

In October of that year, Eliza had her third child, Louise Ezra Cartwright, and John Jr. and Caroline had their second daughter, Ruby E., who was born on December 17, 1876.

In 1877, another cousin was born; her name was Mabel, the only child of Ellen Houghton Jonathan Steinhoff. Ellen had a difficult time naming her daughter. Her head wanted to name her "Jane" after her mother and the sister that she loved. Her heart could not deal with the anguish it felt every time she thought of her dead sister, and having to say "Jane" or "Janie" on a daily basis was beyond her capability. She struggled with a girl's name for the entire pregnancy and eventually her heart won out with the name "Mable," the name of her husband's favorite aunt.

John Houghton with his sisters, 1877.

In 1879, they read in the newspaper about the first telephone call made in the state of Michigan. It was made in Detroit and it was local, of course.

John Jr. and Caroline received a gift three days before Christmas in 1879; her name was Anna Elizabeth, the third girl in the family.

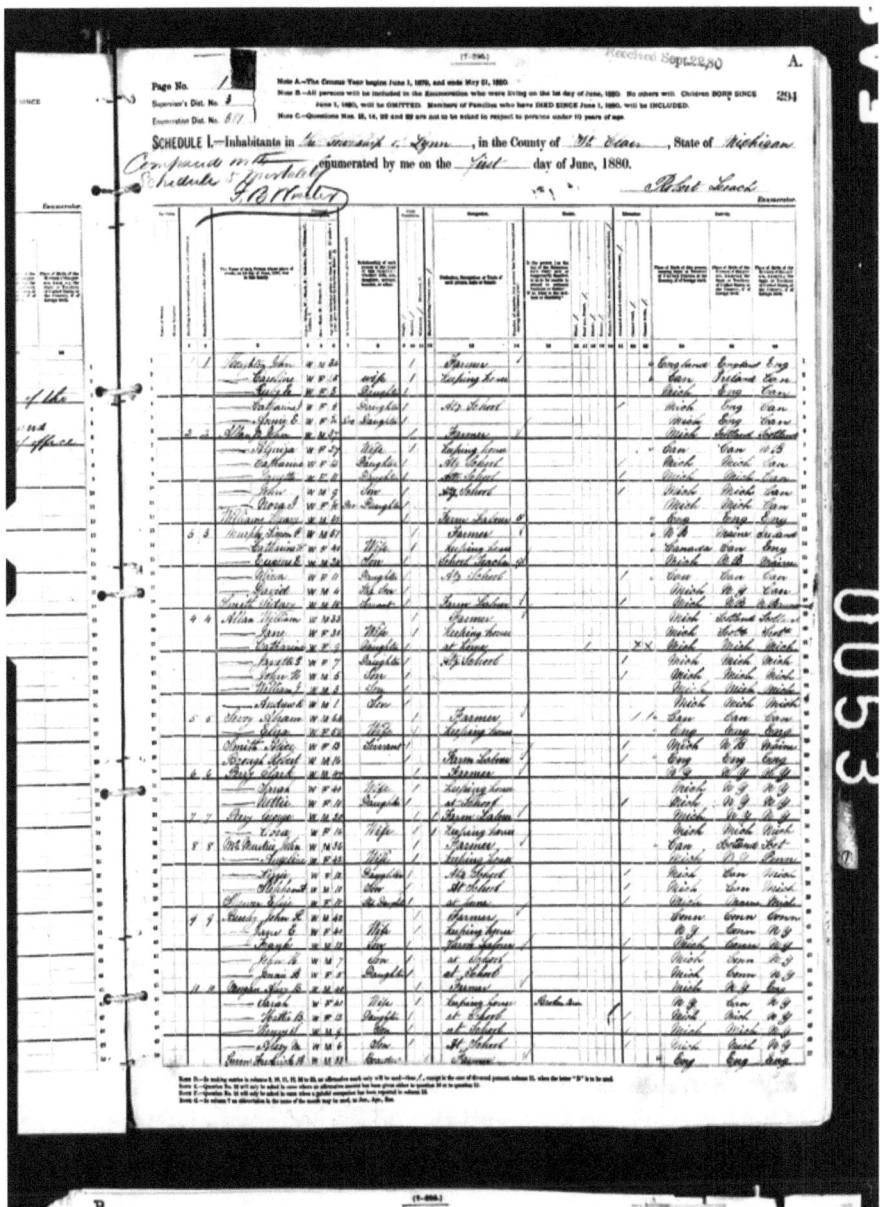

John Jr., Caroline, Ruby, Catherine, and Annie top of page. The 1880 census of Lynn Township.

A New Home

Mt Pleasant, Michigan
1880-1890

John Jr. and his family took part in the 1880 Federal Census and discovered there were now over fifty million people living in the United States, an increase of twenty-seven million people from the time the Houghtons had moved to America. Eliza started the decade with another child, her fourth. She named him William Houghton Cartwright after her grandfather, William Houghton.

* * *

The fire could be seen and the odor of smoke could be smelled from miles away. Another catastrophic fire hit the thumb area of Michigan in 1881, claiming the lives of 282 people and over one million acres of land. The American Red Cross helped the people in the area. This was the first relief effort by the newly formed Red Cross Organization. This fire crippled the thumb area's economy for several years. John, John Jr., and Richard all did what they could to help the victims of the fire.

In 1882, Richard, John's twenty-five-year-old younger brother, was elected as the school inspector on the Republican ticket. Just like clockwork, Eliza had her fifth child, a girl named Alice Bessie. That year John Jr. sold the farm and moved the family to a region that could excite the children's ambition for an education. It was a tearful separation as John Jr., Caroline, and the children waved good-bye from the wagon and headed northwest to their new home. They knew the distance to travel between Lynn and their new home would prevent them from seeing the rest of the family often.

First they traveled on Winn Road for two miles until they reached Shepherd Road. After four miles on Shepherd Road, they turned on what is now called M90 and traveled on it for the rest of the day. They spent the first night at North Branch, making a quick supper and eating around a campfire. When they were finished eating, they cleaned up and John tended to the horses. Caroline made beds under the wagon and after they talked for a while, they crawled into their beds and went to sleep.

The next day they got an early start before the sun came up because it would be the longest part of their trip. They watered and fed the horses at midday in Mayville and spent the night at Vassar.

On day three they woke up to angry-looking skies that were overcast and rainy. The air was invigorating, with a brisk wind coming from the northwest and the skies turning black. The further north they drove, the more they felt they were entering the abyss. The wind and rain became so strong that John unhitched the horses and tied them to a tree. He and the family then got under the wagon and tried to stay dry. Lightning struck all around them and the thunder was so deafening that the horses broke free from the tree and ran off. After the storm, it took John nearly two hours to get the horses back, but they still made it to Saginaw just after sundown and spent the night there.

Day four was a pleasant surprise: the sky was clear, the sun was shining, and the air was fresh from the rain the day before. Everyone was in good spirits. The beautiful rainbow that stretched across the sky that morning reminded them of God's sacred promise that He would never flood the earth again. They viewed the rainbow as a good omen that the rest of the trip would be smooth sailing. This was the first time Catherine Jane, Ruby E., and Anna Elizabeth had ever traveled, and they were having the time of their lives. They spent that night at Merrill and slept hard because they were exhausted.

Day five would bring good weather, and after briefly stopping at Breckenridge to water and feed the horses, they made good time to St. Louis, where they spent the night. The air was cool and got colder because it stormed all night long, which kept everyone awake and made the roads difficult to travel on the next day.

Day six was slow going. The muddy roads made travel excruciatingly time-consuming, and they made it only to the village of Shepherd, where they spent the night. That night the sky was clear and a warm, and a gentle breeze came from the south. John, Caroline, and the girls lay on their backs gazing up at the stars, and John told them about his voyage from England to America. He told them how his mother, sisters, and cousins on the ship used to look for the North Star every night and converse with it because their fathers would speak to it also. The star reminded them of one another. The girls asked their father many questions about his trip to America and then one by one they all drifted off to sleep.

Day seven was sunny again, and by noon the road had dried. They reached their new home, Mecosta, that afternoon and gave thanks to God for bringing them there safely.

1892 Land contract in Union Township, Mt. Pleasant, Michigan, between C. Bennett and John Jr. Houghton.

On November 10, 1892, John Jr. moved the family to Union Township. This included the city of Mt. Pleasant, which had only about a thousand inhabitants when they moved there. He paid twelve hundred dollars for the land and home. Their forty-acre farm was in the country, north of the U.S. Indian Industrial School. The farm no longer exists and is part of the city now.

The children were in school district 8 and had about a three-mile walk to their schoolhouse. A schoolteacher earned twenty-five dollars a month for teaching two grades, forty dollars a month for teaching three grades, and fifty dollars a month for teaching four grades.

Emma, John's younger sister, followed him north in 1883 and married Daniel Mac Lachlan in Mt. Pleasant, Michigan. John Jr.'s younger brother Richard Henry, twenty-seven, got married in 1884 in Lynn to Cora Hollenbeck and helped farm the old homestead.

Maud Caroline was born on August 4, 1884 in Mecosta to John Jr. and Caroline. John Jr.'s family now had four girls: Catherine, nine; Ruby, seven; Anna, four; and newly born Maud.

On July 9, 1885, Richard Henry had his first child, a boy, Herbert John. If Richard had lived in Detroit, he could have made a long-distance phone call to any major city up to a hundred miles away and made the announcement. It was possible to call Saginaw, Flint, Lansing, Ann Arbor, and Toledo, Ohio from Detroit.

The Indian Wars officially ended on September 4, 1886 when Geronimo surrendered at Fort Bowie in Arizona. One month later, John Jr. received a telegram that Great-Great-Great-Grandfather William had died. The Houghtons arranged with their neighbors to watch their livestock while they were gone for the funeral.

They went to the train station in Mt. Pleasant and boarded the Owosso and Northwestern railroad headed to Owosso. At Owosso, they changed trains and boarded the Huron and Lake Michigan railroad headed to Capac. When they reached Capac, they rented a buggy at the livery and rode the eight miles to Lynn. The trip was about 170 miles but took most of the day and they got to Lynn late that night.

1868

Great-Great-Great-Grandfather William

1792-1886

Great-Great-Great-Grandfather William Houghton worked on the farm until the day he died, and he rarely ventured farther from the farm than the distance a horse or buggy could take him in a day.

Through the years, he frequently wrote to his wife Elizabeth, who still lived in England. He missed her and talked about their lives together in Lincolnshire. He missed the way she used to cook and the way she slept next to him on a cold night. He never blamed her for not coming to America. He never would have forgiven himself if she had attempted the trip and did not make it. He missed her voice and the way she used to call him "William" in her thick brogue. To him there was no better woman on the face of the earth than Elizabeth, so he never attempted to remarry in America.

One day a letter came from his daughter Mary telling him that Elizabeth had died. Before she died, she asked Mary to write to William and tell him that she would love him until the end of time, and she was looking forward to that great reunion day when they would reunite in heaven and spend eternity together.

Before his death, William reminisced about his life to the children living on the farm. He said, "I have searched my past from the mountain of old age, and I can see all of my accomplishments with the clarity of hindsight.

"In my life," he said, "there have been heartache and pain, joy and happiness, disappointments and many surprises, but there is nothing I would change. I believe my purpose in life was to establish my family in America, and I have accomplished that and God has blessed us."

As the day drew closer to William's death, John said that William looked every bit the ninety-four years he was. He used a cane to walk and his eyes were growing dimmer with each passing year. Jane could see the care of the world in his eyes and an accumulation of life's worries on his furrowed brow.

William remained physically fit even with over nine decades of life under his belt. Everyone commented that he was as strong as a bull, probably from digging wells most of his life and farming. William seldom missed a chance to prove his strength by arm-wrestling younger men, "young bucks" as he called them, and he won more often than not.

William was healthy all the days of his life until he died in his sleep at the age of ninety-four years, one month, and three days. He died on October 13, 1886 and is buried in the Lynn Cemetery.

STATE OF MICHIGAN
County of St. Clair
Port Huron, Michigan

DEATH RECORD
ISSUED BY
MARILYN DUNN
COUNTY CLERK
ST. CLAIR COUNTY, PORT HURON, MICHIGAN
OF
WILLIAM HOUGHTON

CERTIFIED COPY OF DEATH RECORD

I, MARILYN DUNN, Clerk of the County of St. Clair and of the Circuit Court thereof, the same being a Court of Record having a Seal, do hereby certify that the following is a copy of the Record of Death of

WILLIAM HOUGHTON , now remaining in my office, viz:

FULL NAME OF THE DECEASED: WILLIAM HOUGHTON

RECORD NO.	DATE OF DEATH			DATE OF BIRTH			Age of Deceased		
	Month	Date	Year	Month	Date	Year	Years	Months	Days
2-175	October	--	1886	-------	--	----	94	1	3

Male Or Female	White, Black Mulatto, Etc.	Marital Status	Name of Informant	Address
Male	White	Widower	--------	----------

PLACE OF DEATH	BIRTH PLACE OF DECEASED	OCCUPATION OF DECEASED
Lynn	England	Farmer

FATHER'S NAME	Birthplace or Residency	MOTHER'S NAME	Birthplace or Residency
Unknown	Unknown	Unknown	Unknown

CAUSE OF DEATH
Unknown

DATE RECORDED: June 27, 1887

In Testimony Whereof, I have hereunto set my hand and affixed the seal of the of the Circuit Court, this 27th day of March   A. D. 2009,

MARILYN DUNN   County Clerk,

By _____ Deputy Clerk

The winter of 1886 was unusually cold and harsh. Many people were killed by the snowstorms and the cattle industry was decimated, driving up the price of beef for years. After 1886, free-grazing cattle became a thing of the past. John and Caroline were blessed, and they did not lose one animal to the storms that year.

In 1888, the family became two people larger. On December 15, 1888, Richard Henry had his second child, Sara (Sadie) Jane, and Eliza had her sixth child, Ethel May.

By 1890, a farmer was three times more productive than he had been in 1850. A farmer with a riding gangplow and four good horses could plow six acres in a day. Before the riding plow, an average farmer with three horses pulling a one-bottom 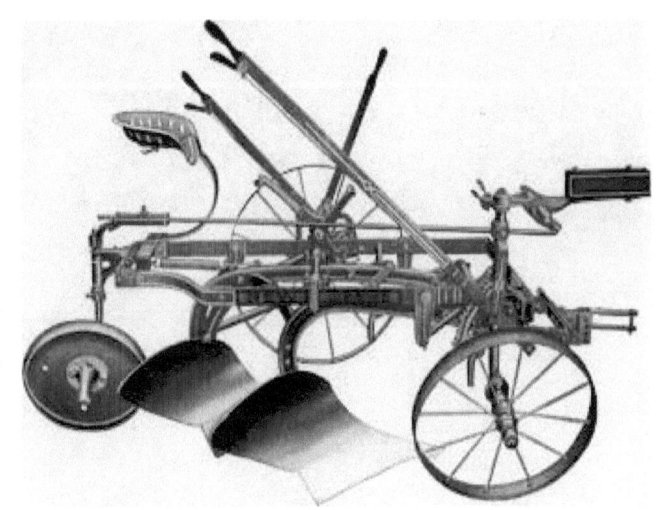 walking plow could break only two acres a day. It used to take ninety hours of labor to produce a hundred bushels of corn, and now it took only forty hours.

The village of Mt. Pleasant was growing rapidly, and in 1892, Central Michigan Normal School and Business opened its doors. It would later be called Central Michigan University.

John Jr. Houghton, 1896.

PLACE OF BIRTH				MICHIGAN	
County of	Isabella			DEPARTMENT OF HEALTH	
or				Bureau of Records and Statistics	
Twp. Of	Union			CERTIFICATE OF BIRTH	
or					Register No.	896
City of	Mt. Pleasant				Lib. 3 Pge. 137
				Name of Hospital or Institution	

FULL NAME OF CHILD		John Donald Houghton			
Sex Male	If plural Births	single	Legitimate Full Term	Date of Birth	January 5, 1893
Full Name John Houghton	Father		Full Maiden Name Carrie Houghton	Mother	
Residence Union Twp			Union Twp		
Color White	Age Not Listed		Color White	Age Not Listed	
Birthplace England			Birthplace Canada		
Occupation Farmer			Occupation Not Listed		
Number of child of this mother	N/A		Number of children, of this mother, now living		N/A

CERTIFICATE OF ATTENDING PHYSICIAN OR MIDWIFE

I hereby certify that I attended the birth of this child who was born alive on the date above stated.

	(Signature)	Not Listed
Have eyes of child been treated with 1 1/2% solution of silver nitrate as required	N/A	Dated	Not Listed
		Address	Not Listed
		Filed May 12, 1894

STATE OF MICHIGAN } ss
COUNTY OF ISABELLA }

I do HEREBY CERTIFY that this is a true and correct copy of the certificate for the person named therin as it now appears in the permanent records of the Isabella County Clerk's Office. This record is not valid without the raised seal of this department.

_3-18-09_   Joyce A. Swan
Date   Joyce A. Swan
                   Isabella County Clerk

John III Houghton's birth certificate. January 5, 1893.

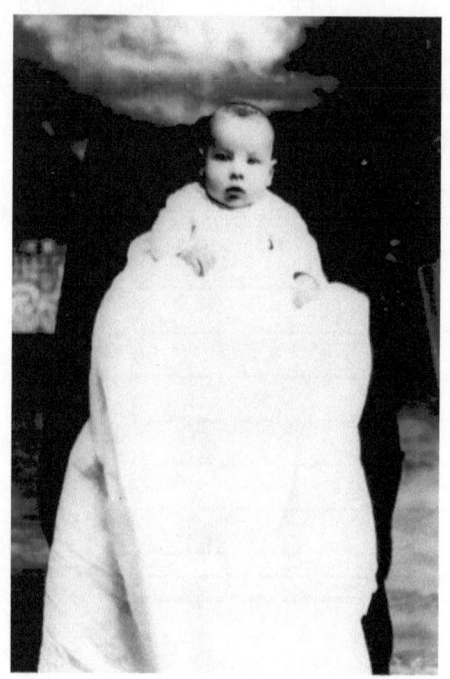

John III Houghton, 1893. John III Houghton, 1896.

John III Donald Houghton

1893

John Jr. lived in a household full of women. His only son had died as an infant, and even though he never said it aloud, you could sense his frustration that the family line and name would end with him. Nearly eight years had passed since the birth of his last child, Maud.

Spring was here. John Jr. came into the house from tending the cattle, and Caroline called him to the kitchen, asking him to sit down. Caroline was looking concerned, and John Jr. asked her what was wrong. Caroline began to cry and said, "God is so good, He has blessed us with another child." John Jr. could not believe his ears and asked her to repeat what she said. She repeated, "I'm going to have a baby." John looked stunned and then began to weep as he hugged Caroline. He then knelt in front of her, touched her belly, and prayed that God would keep his unborn child safe and healthy.

On January 4, a midwife came over to the Houghton house to help Caroline have her baby. At 3:05 in the morning on January 5, 1893, John Jr. heard the cries of a baby coming from their bedroom. The midwife called John Jr. into the room to see Caroline holding the baby wrapped in a blanket. As John Jr. stepped closer to look at the baby, Caroline opened the blanket and revealed to him his new son. John Jr. was so full of emotion he could not hold back the tears.

John and Caroline's last baby was Grandfather John III. To say John III was indulged as a child would be an understatement. There were almost nineteen years between the oldest and youngest children. There were now four girls and one boy in the family. John III often remarked that his older sisters were lucky because they had only one mother, but he had five: Caroline, Catherine, Ruby, Anna, and Maud.

John III with sisters Ruby, Maud, Anna, and Catherine. 1897

The worst depression of the 19th century began in 1893, but John Jr. was a farmer, and farmers had food on the table regardless of the economy. By now, the farm was fully operational and the girls helped John plow the fields and tend the livestock. All the girls got a complete education and graduated from high school.

In 1895 John and Caroline's nest would start to empty when Ruby E., now nineteen, married Lester Drew. They had a large celebration and all the family from downstate was able to attend the wedding.

In 1896, the family received a telegram with the heartbreaking news that Great-Great-Grandmother Jane had died. Nearly every person in the township turned out for her funeral. John Jr. and his family took the train to Lynn. By now, the eight-day journey had been reduced to just a day.

Great-Great-Grandmother Jane

1819-1896

Great-Great-Grandmother Jane was the loving matriarch who brought strength to every life she touched. She was a faithful wife, mother, and member of the Methodist Episcopal Church, and I know that heaven is a better place because she is there.

On the sunny fall morning of September 17, 1896, she died in John's arms. They were alone in their home, and John sat with her for the longest time after her death, just stoking her hair and talking to her. Even in death, she was the most beautiful woman he had ever seen. They would quickly pass from each other's sight, but John knew that when he saw Jane again, there would be heaven. He wondered how he had been so lucky that an angel would want to spend her life with him.

John went through a gauntlet of emotions for over a month, sad that she was gone but happy that she was now free in heaven. His emotions were shackled to an enormous wall of memories; memories that haunted him, and memories that set him free. The haunting came from the realization that he did not utilize every moment he had with

Jane to its fullest. The freeing came from the knowledge that they deeply loved one another and would some day reunite. How could he carry on? His best girl, the love of his life, the only woman he had ever loved, was gone.

He reminisced about the first time he lost his heart to Jane, the day he knew he would never be complete unless she married him. It was summer and he was at Jane's parents' house in England. Everyone was outside standing around a campfire, taking turns poking at the fire and watching specs of red ash float into the dark night. It was a cool night without a cloud in the sky. John looked up and caught Jane looking at him across the campfire, and she smiled. For the first time his eyes were open—she had been right there in front of him nearly all his life, but he had never seen her until that night. He knew then that she was the one for him forever.

As the flames flickered, the faces warmed, and everyone stared into the fire, John heard a dog howl and looked up into the enormous black bowl of shimmering stars, the constellations standing out as clearly as he had ever seen them. He watched a single star break free, looping downward as it trailed a long, silvery tail that briefly sliced the sky. It wasn't just the stars that night that fell for Jane's beauty, and John never saw his heart again until it broke with Jane's passing.

John learned many things from Jane over their fifty-one years of marriage. She was a woman and a creature of the heart; what he thought, she felt. He learned from her how to tap that feeling side of his brain and became a better man for it.

He lost a little vigor in his step after her death, and he often talked about that grand homecoming day when he and Jane would be together again. John's pain was tempered by the fact that he could see Jane's face in all the things she loved the most: the flowers she grew every year, the sunset, and the faces of their grandchildren.

Jane and John often walked to Mill Creek and sat under the shade of the old oak tree where Janie was buried. It had become their favorite place on the farm. After Jane's death John continued to visit that spot, and he would spend hours thinking about a time when he wore a younger man's clothes, how Jane and he had lived their lives, shared their love with one another, and raised their family together. There were times while sitting next to the river that he thought he saw Jane's reflection in the water. It seemed so real to him and brought him much comfort. He would talk to Jane while he sat there, and he would always tell her that he loved her as he got up and walked back to the house. John knew she was gone, but he also knew that the day they would reunite was coming quickly.

Jane was buried at Lynn Cemetery. I have mixed feelings about mourning someone that you must so quickly follow. Death touches us all and is a natural part of living. From the day of our birth, we are all on the path leading to it; none of us is getting out of here alive.

Later that year, in 1896, Catherine Jane, who was twenty-two and John Jr.'s oldest daughter, married Sylvester Baughman at Mt. Pleasant and moved to Shepherd, Michigan.

By 1898, there were 30,000 telephones in use in Michigan, and smaller towns like Mt. Pleasant had a twenty to thirty-mile radius in which they could make calls. John Jr. didn't have a phone yet, but a general store not far from the house did. They could call a general store in Shepherd and leave messages for Catherine. This was a huge timesaver and well worth the three cents it cost to place the call.

In September of 1898, fourteen-year-old Maud walked her little brother John III to the one-room schoolhouse for the first time and introduced him to the teacher and the rest of his schoolmates. John liked school and books and took to his studies like a duck to water. He did so well his first year that he was moved up an extra grade, skipping first grade altogether. John's mother kept his hair long when he was younger and this would require several fights at school to prove to the other boys that he was all boy and capable of holding his own.

John Jr., Maud, Catherine, John III, Ruby, Anna, and Caroline Houghton. 1900

1900 Federal Census Isabella County, Union Township. John Jr. and Caroline at the bottom of page.

The family took part in another census in 1900 that revealed a population of nearly seventy-six million people in the United States. The industrial revolution was fully engaged and farmers were now only 38% of the labor force. In this year, Anna Elizabeth, John Jr's third daughter, married Parker Atwell. This left Maud and John III, who was now seven, the only children at home with John Jr. and Caroline.

The family read in the paper later that year that William McKinley had been elected for his second term, with Theodore Roosevelt as his vice president. Anna Elizabeth had seven grandchildren for John Jr., and Anna's first child was born in 1901. She named him Steven.

John III had just started fourth grade when his class read about the assassination attempt on President McKinley by Leon Czolgoz on September 6. President McKinley was wounded and would die on September 14, and Theodore Roosevelt would be sworn in as president on the same day. John's school was closed for two days in honor of the president.

Football was beginning to make its way into the American culture, and on January 1, 1902, the first Rose Bowl game was played in Pasadena, California between Michigan and Stanford Universities. Stanford was being beaten so badly by Michigan, 49-0, that Stanford quit the game in the third quarter and left the field. John III read to his father about the results of the game the day before his ninth birthday.

John III heard about something new called "the airplane" while he was at school. His class read an article about the different inventors trying to become like the birds and fly. Just before Christmas on December 17, 1903, his class was captivated by the news of Orville Wright and his 120-foot flight in twelve seconds.

Elizabeth

A Shining Light
1861-1904

Elizabeth—or Lizzie, as everyone called her—was John Jr.'s youngest sister. She became a teacher and taught for a while on an Indian reservation out west. She married Robert Shutt, and they were unable to have children. She was in charge of a young women's detention home for many years until she moved back to Lynn, Michigan.

Elizabeth was artistic and her passion was sketching and painting. As a young woman, she read about Leonardo da Vinci and the theory of the golden mean. The golden mean is a mathematical formula that painters use in composing paintings; it contains complex math used to draw human figures. It dates from the Renaissance and is still used today, although today you might hear it called the 'rule of thirds'.

The theory was something that resonated inside Elizabeth and touched her soul.

Her favorite subjects to paint were people. She painted people to get a better feeling of who they were; their facial expressions, their eyes, their smile or lack thereof, made them more real to her. Most of Elizabeth's paintings were done while she was the headmistress of the young woman's detention school. Some of her favorite subjects to paint were the young women who were the most difficult to get along with in the school. They were the young women who pushed the rules to their limits and often broke them; they attempted to run away from the school and they required extra attention, instruction, discipline, and love.

Most of her painting at the school took place in the Enforcer, a room in the school that looked like a jail cell. It was fourteen by fourteen feet, with two sets of bunk beds and one wooden table with four chairs. Across the front of the room were bars that made everything inside it visible. A window with bars across it on the back wall could open to the outside.

Only the most difficult young women ever saw this room, but everyone in the school knew it was there. No one wanted to spend time in the Enforcer, and just the thought of going there helped impose the rules of the school.

Elizabeth used the time while painting the young women to discuss anything and everything. The painting disarmed the young women and usually made them more open to talking. Elizabeth used the paintings as a tutorial to teach the young women a little about life.

Elizabeth's favorite painting is of three young women who became familiar with the Enforcer. She invested many hours of herself into these three while they were at the school. The painting shows the young women sitting together on the bottom bunk in the Enforcer. It is dark outside, but three candles light the room. The middle young woman has a Bible in her lap and it is open; the young women on either side of her are leaning slightly forward in front of her, straining to see what she has just read. The young woman on the left has her hand on the Bible and is pointing to the scripture the young woman in the middle has just read; it is John 3:16-21:

#

For God so loved the world that he gave his one and only Son, that whoever believes in him shall not perish but have eternal life. For God did not send his Son into the world to condemn the world but to save the world through him. Whoever believes in him is not condemned, but whoever does not believe stands condemned already because he has not believed in the name of God's one and only Son. This is the verdict: Light has come into the world, but men loved darkness instead of light because their deeds were evil. Everyone who does evil hates the light; and will not come into the light for fear that his deeds will be exposed. But whoever lives by the truth comes into the light, so that it may be seen plainly that what he has done has been done through God.

#

The middle young woman is looking up and has tears flowing down her cheeks; her expression is one of amazement. She is staring at the only window in the room, and even though it is dark outside, the window has a bright light shining through it. The shafts of light from the window are shinning directly on the Bible; three birds are on the window and it is open. Two of the birds are getting ready to fly, and the third one is caught in mid-flight, heading outside towards the light and freedom. Elizabeth named the painting "Released from Captivity."

After finishing the painting, she explained the scripture to the young women and then talked about the painting. "The three candles in the room represent the Father, Son, and Holy Spirit and give the light. The light from the window represents the Holy Spirit and He is shining on the Word of God that is bringing truth and revelation to the young women and setting them free. The three birds on the window are  the three young women; the two getting ready to fly are the two on either side of the middle young woman trying to read the Bible passage. The third bird is the middle young woman, who has just seen the truth and is now flying free into the light."

After she shared her thoughts with them about the painting, they all cried together. God used the painting to touch the young women so deeply that they were never inside the Enforcer again.

All three young women came from different backgrounds, and all had been wounded in many different ways. They all had something in common: a deep void that they tried to fill with many different things—relationships, money, sex, and food. However, today they had realized that the void could be filled only by Jesus Christ. Every other thing they tried to fill it with eventually let them down. The middle young woman in the painting later became a teacher and stayed in touch with Elizabeth the rest of Elizabeth's life.

John Jr. got a telegram in 1904 from his father telling him that Elizabeth had died. Once again, the family took the train trip to Capac and rented the buggy for the eight-mile drive to Lynn. John Jr. and his family attended the funeral and used the remainder of their time there to become reacquainted with family and friends.

Elizabeth was involved in a buggy accident, which took her life at the age of forty-three. She was driving her buggy when her horse was spooked by the backfire of a horseless carriage; the buggy got away from her and overturned, throwing her into a tree and killing her instantly.

The family received letters from women Elizabeth had had as students over the years, thanking her for what she had done for them. Several weeks after the funeral, the family heard a knock at their front door. It was Samantha Jackson, the young woman in the painting *Released from Captivity*. She kept in touch with Elizabeth after leaving school and said she had to make the pilgrimage to Elizabeth's grave to pay her respects. Samantha shared her side of the story behind the painting and what profound change it brought to her life. "Elizabeth," she said, "was an angel wearing skin and now she has her wings."

Also in 1904, Theodore Roosevelt, the former Rough Rider, was elected president by a landslide over Democratic candidate Alton B. Parker. Theodore, who spent some time in the West as a young man, had a vision for the county's national parks and set aside enormous sections of land for future generations to enjoy.

The Houghton family did not own an automobile yet, but it was becoming evident to everyone that there needed to be laws passed to regulate their drivers' behavior. The first speed limit for automobiles was passed in New York in 1904, setting the speed limit at ten miles per hour in the city and twenty miles per hour in the country.

Great-Great-Grandfather John

1824-1906

John Jr. received another telegram on January 16, 1906, telling him that his father had passed away. The entire family attended the funeral at Lynn. Grandfather John III was now thirteen; the trip to Lynn was his fourth on a train, and John III was beginning to associate the train with death.

Great-Great-Grandfather John was popular in the community and there was no building big enough to hold all the people that turned out for his funeral. Great-Great-Grandfather John was written about in the Biographical Memoirs of Saint Clair County, Michigan, published in 1903 by B.F. Publishers in Logansport, Indiana. The biography spans two pages, 476-477. Here are a couple of excerpts from that book:

#

Few English-born agriculturists in Lynn Township are better known or more highly respected than John Houghton. He filled the office of township supervisor for ten years, of which seven were in consecutive order; for two years, he was Drain Commissioner and served one term as constable and four as town treasurer. Mr. Houghton is the oldest living settler in Lynn Township. Mr. Houghton is highly respected for his unswerving integrity, his public spirit, and his many sterling traits of personal character.

#

"He inspires me to be like him."

#

Before his death, John said he met Him when he was a young man. He was a man's man, someone who was not afraid to be strong but could be touched by compassion and show his compassion with a tear when met by loss. John loved Him more than he loved anyone he had ever known other than Jane, his wife. The more he got to know Him the more he fell in love with Him. John said, "He inspires me to be like Him and to be a better person."

John's special friend was his Lord and savior Jesus Christ. "The first thing I would like to hear when I meet him face-to-face," John said, "is, 'well done, thou good and faithful servant.'"

Great-Great-Grandfather John was a risk-taker, a good father, and a faithful member of the Methodist Episcopal Church. He was a compassionate, tolerant man who had the willingness to overlook mistakes. John's life reflected the heart of the Son of Man, who did not come to be served but to serve, and to give his life. John was confident of one thing: he who began a good work in Him would be faithful to bring it to completion.

After all the years he lived in America, he never lost his British accent. He died from septic anemia on January 16, 1906 and is buried at Lynn Cemetery next to his wife, Jane.

The original settlers, the innovative pioneers, the imaginative risk-takers of our family have passed. They risked everything—even their lives—to give us a better life. We will forever be indebted to them, and I for one am grateful for their lives and sacrifice.

STATE OF MICHIGAN
County of St. Clair
Port Huron, Michigan

DEATH RECORD
ISSUED BY
MARILYN DUNN
COUNTY CLERK
ST. CLAIR COUNTY, PORT HURON, MICHIGAN
OF
JOHN HOUGHTON

CERTIFIED COPY OF DEATH RECORD

I, **MARILYN DUNN**, Clerk of the County of St. Clair and of the Circuit Court thereof, the same being a Court of Record having a Seal, do hereby certify that the following is a copy of the Record of Death of

JOHN HOUGHTON _____, now remaining in my office, viz:

FULL NAME OF THE DECEASED: JOHN HOUGHTON

RECORD NO.	DATE OF DEATH			DATE OF BIRTH			Age of Deceased		
	Month	Date	Year	Month	Date	Year	Years	Months	Days
4-67	January	16	1906	------	--	----	81	6	21

Male Or Female	White, Black Mulatto, Etc.	Marital Status	Name of Informant	Address
Male	White	Widowed	--------	----------

PLACE OF DEATH	BIRTH PLACE OF DECEASED	OCCUPATION OF DECEASED
Lynn	England	Farmer

FATHER'S NAME	Birthplace or Residency	MOTHER'S NAME	Birthplace or Residency
William Houghton	Lynn	Elizabeth Burns	--------

CAUSE OF DEATH

Septic Anemia

DATE RECORDED: _____ March 8, 1906 _____

In Testimony Whereof, I have hereunto set my hand and affixed the seal of the of the Circuit Court, this 27th day of _____ March _____ A. D. 2009,

MARILYN DUNN   County Clerk,

By _____   Deputy Clerk

A New Century

Mt. Pleasant, Michigan
1900-1920

Anna Elizabeth made John Jr. and Caroline grandparents again with the birth of her second child, Ross Lincoln Atwell, in 1903. Herbert John Houghton, Richard Henry's son, got married to Janet Cameron (born 1884) in Lynn. Richard Henry never left the farm in Lynn and lived with his father and mother until their death. He inherited the old homestead and added another eighty acres to it. Now Richard and his son Herbert were both living on the 320-acre farm, and making a living together.

Anna Elizabeth started the year 1906 with the birth of her third child on January 16, a boy they named Wayne Ellis Atwell.

In 1908, Anna Elizabeth paid tribute to her father by naming her fourth child John Houghton Atwell. In politics that year, Republican candidate William Taft was elected president over his Democratic rival, William Bryan.

The year 1910 was a busy one for the Houghtons with the marriage of Sara H., Richard Henry's daughter, to Robert Martin (born August 1888) on January 5 in Yale, Michigan. Later that year, Sara would have an early Christmas gift with the birth of James Houghton Martin on December 1.

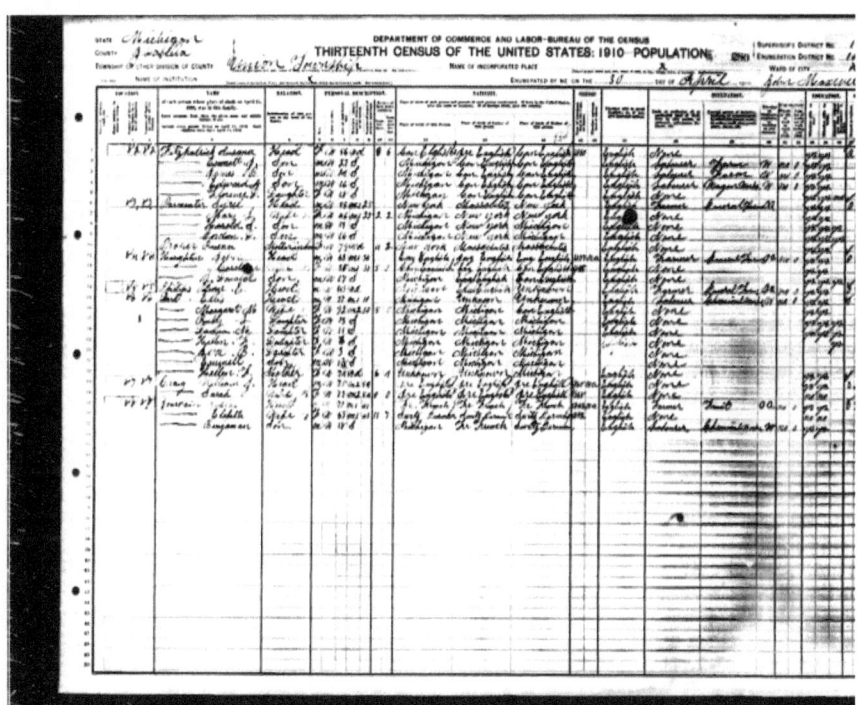

1910 Federal Census. Union Township Isabella county, Michigan. John II, Caroline, and John III.

The Houghton family participated in the 1910 census and discovered that there were nearly ninety-two million people living in America. Farmers made up only 31% of the labor force, and the average farm measured 138 acres. Anna Elizabeth (Houghton) Atwell would add another citizen to America with the birth of her fifth child, Mary Jane Atwell, just before Christmas.

New Mexico became a state on January 6, 1912 and was quickly followed by Arizona, which was admitted to the Union on February 14,

1912. The star count on the flag was now forty-eight; this flag would fly over the United States for forty-seven years through two world wars, and eight presidents would serve under it.

During the week of April 15, 1912, the only thing everyone was talking about was the sinking of the *Titanic*. News bulletins about the sinking came in all week long and people could not get enough information about the particulars of the catastrophe.

The Houghton family experienced a death, a birth, and a marriage in 1912. Ruby E. had bad news for the family when her husband Lester died. Anna Elizabeth brightened up the year with the birth of her sixth child, Donald. Ruby E. wasted no time getting remarried to Charles Gray, a railroad engineer from Winnipeg in the Canadian province of Ontario. She would make her home in Canada from then on.

The year 1913 was a bad one for all Americans with the passage of the Sixteenth Amendment, which provided a graduated national tax. The wealthy, with all their loopholes, found a way to get the masses to pay for roads and other infrastructure projects so they could better enjoy America.

John Jr. bought his first car in 1914 while World War I was raging in Europe, a Model T Ford that cost him $575. The salesperson told John he could have any color he wanted as long as it was black, so he chose the black model.

Three more children were born this year. The first one was Helen C. Martin, born to Sara, the daughter of Richard Henry. Second was Helen Caroline, born to Ruby (Houghton) Gray in Winnipeg, Canada, and the third was Ruth Atwell, daughter of Anna Elizabeth (Houghton) Atwell. Ruth was Anna's seventh and last child; her thirteen years of childbearing were over, and she said, "Amen."

In 1916, Woodrow Wilson won reelection on the campaign slogan: "He kept us out of the war." Five months later, on April 2, 1917, President Wilson asked Congress to declare war on Germany, saying, "The world must be made safe for democracy." John III was twenty-four years old and had to sign up for the draft, but his number was never called and he did not serve in the military. By 1917, John III was already married and had two children.

John Jr. and Caroline lived on their farm outside Mt. Pleasant, Michigan until 1918. They then moved to Shepherd, Michigan in 1918 to live with their oldest daughter, Catherine (Houghton) Baughman. The year 1918 saw the largest influenza outbreak the world has ever known. Over fifty million people died worldwide— 670,000 in the United States.

John II, Caroline
1906.

John and Caroline escaped the epidemic and spent the remainder of their life living with their daughter Catherine.

John Jr. died on May 10, 1920 and was buried at Riverside Cemetery in Mt. Pleasant, Michigan. Caroline died in 1946 and is buried next to him.

John III, Blanche with Jack and Eleanor, 1917.   **Blanche (Taylor) Houghton, 1910.**

Blanche (Taylor) Houghton far left, 1908.

John III and Blanche Houghton

The World Is Quickly Changing

John III was born in Mt. Pleasant and was raised there. He was a handsome man, tall and slender. He was quiet-natured, intelligent, hard-working, and a stern disciplinarian. John III would live through the greatest birth of technology the world has ever known. His life would see the change from horse and buggy to rockets to the moon.

He met Blanche Mary Taylor when he was twenty years old and fell in love. Blanche was short with a thin frame, kind and gentle and in all ways generous and godly. John and Blanche got married on August

30, 1914 in Mt. Pleasant. They lived in Lincoln Township for a while before moving to Hillman, Michigan.

In 1922, they moved to Detroit, Michigan, and John III started a contracting business there. They lived in Wayne County, the city of Detroit, precinct 67, block 88. John and Blanche would have seven children:

1. Eleanor Loretta (October 30, 1915–September 12, 1992)

2. John Donald (October 15, 1916–April 12, 2007)

3. Lee Maurice (born September 1918)

4. Welbie Elton (October 21, 1920–March 30, 2009)

5. William Dale (September 5, 1924–May 9, 1996)

6. Blanch Elaine (born 1928)

7. Kenneth Scott (born August 27, 1935)

William, Eleanor, Kenneth, Welbie, Elaine, Jack, Blanche, and John III 1940. Taken on the Houghton farm.

The Houghton Seven

On October 30, 1915, John III and Blanche had their first child, Eleanor Loretta Houghton. She would be the first in the family in many ways. She was first to be born, first to get married, first to have children, and first to die. She was like a second mother to all her siblings.

My father remembers Mother's Day of 1929, when they lived in Detroit. Eleanor was given a nickel by her father with instructions to help five-year-old William buy a gift for their mother for Mother's Day. Eleanor helped William pick out a ceramic elephant figurine that had a pincushion on its back. William had hoped that there might be some money left over from the nickel to buy some candy, but the figurine cost exactly five cents. William swelled with pride when he gave his mother the figurine on

Eleanor , William 1926

Mother's Day. The figurine has survived many moves over the years in one piece and today sits in my own china cabinet.

Eleanor married Leroy Nelson on October 18, 1933 in Mt. Pleasant, Michigan. They built a home next to the Chippewa River down the road from the Houghton farm. They farmed and owned a grain mill. Leroy and Eleanor had two children, Loretta and Leroy Jr.

Eleanor was spontaneous, and I remember her driving over to our house often just to chat. One time she came to the house to show off her good fortune. She had a thousand-dollar bill and showed it to everyone. This was in 1962 when the government still made thousand-dollar bills, before they were banned because of money laundering by drug cartels. Eleanor placed the bill on top of the television and talked to everyone for quite some time. When she was done conversing, she got in her car and drove home, forgetting the thousand dollars on the television.

When Eleanor realized what she had done, she was back at our house faster than the roadrunner being chased by Wile E. Coyote. Eleanor died on September 12, 1992 and was buried at Two Rivers Cemetery.

In the year 1916, World War I was still going on in Europe, and John III and Blanche were getting ready for the arrival of their second child. John Donald Jr. was born on October 30, 1916 in Lincoln Township. John Jr. went by the name of Jack, thus extending the Houghton tradition of

Eleanor, Welbie, Jack, and Lee, 1925.

going by a name other then their given first name. Also born in 1916 was Margaret Ruth Martin to Sara, the daughter of Richard Henry Houghton.

Jack farmed on his father's farm and became a carpenter and bricklayer. He married Jean Sparks during World War II in August of 1943.

Jack was the last of the four boys to go into the Marines during the war. He was twenty-eight and considered the old man among all the eighteen-year-olds in the service. He went on to fight at Okinawa, Japan with the Fifth Marines.

After the war, Jack and Jean would be one of three Houghton children to build their home on the fringes of the Houghton farm. Their home was next to Lee and Jean's on the west end of the property. They had four children: Mary, Nora, John, and Janet. John died on April 12, 2007.

John III and Blanche's third child was another boy, named Lee Maurice. He was born in September of 1918 in Lincoln Township. Lee continued the family tradition of going by a name other than his given name, and everyone called him Maurice. Richard Henry Houghton's wife Cora died this year at the age of sixty. On November 11, the family rejoiced when they heard on the radio that World War I had ended with Germany signing the armistice treaty.

Lee was the first of the boys to go into the Marines during World War II. He left for the corps in February 1942. He fought at Okinawa, Japan and was wounded there. He contracted amoebic dysentery while at Guam, which required medical attention. After the war was over, he was shipped to the Great Lakes Medical Hospital in Milwaukee, Wisconsin and remained there until he was discharged from the service in February 1946. While he was living in Milwaukee, he met and fell in love with Eugenia (Jean) Janus, and he married her in February 1946.

He returned to the farm with his bride, and they built a home next to Jack and Jean on the west end of the Houghton property. Lee eventually became a bricklayer, like his father. Jean and Lee would have three children, Lynn, Lee Jr., and Brian.

Aunts and uncles of the family were getting older, and as time passed so came the inevitable. Herbert Houghton's wife Janet died at the age of thirty-six in Flint, Michigan in 1920, the same year that Great-Grandpa John Jr. passed. Eliza, John Jr.'s youngest sister, died on January 10, 1921. She was seventy-three years old.

Welbie Elton Houghton was born on October 21, 1920 in Hillman, Michigan. Welbie joined the Marines during WWII on March 23, 1942 with his younger brother William and never returned to the farm to live.

After the war, he joined his wife Betty (Clark) and his daughter Daya in Ithaca, New York. Betty and Welbie were married during the war in August 1944. Welbie became a bricklayer, like his father, and they lived in New York, Texas, and Florida. During the war, Welbie and William spent the first two years together in California, Hawaii, and the Midway Islands.

Welbie and William made a pact during their time in the service to name their first boy after each other, and they did. Welbie and Betty had four children: Daya, William, Joy, and John. Welbie's son William named his two boys Welbie and William. To keep the tradition of a Houghton not going by his or her given first name (Grandpa John III and six of the seven children went by names other than their given first name), Betty called Uncle Welbie "Jim".

The decision to name me after my Uncle Welbie was made by my father during WWII. Because of the name connection Uncle Welbie always had a special place in my heart. I did not see him often because he always lived a good distance from us in other states. When he did visit there was always a family get together planned to celebrate his homecoming. He always came with his family and there would be many activities planned while they were visiting.

Shortly after Grandma Houghton's death, Uncle Welbie visited Michigan by himself to go on a fishing trip to Canada with his brothers and father. He took the bus and we picked him up at the bus station. Before they left for their fishing trip Uncle Welbie and I had some time alone. This was the first and last time this ever happened. We talked about the unusual name we both shared. Welbie is an old English name that means *farm by the brook*.

Uncle Welbie shared with me the story of his time with my father during WWII, how they gave their word to one another to name their first boy after each other. He confided in me that my father was always his closest sibling and told me about some of the things they did during the war.

The mood was light and I was enjoying our conversation. Then Uncle Welbie got serious and told me about his time at Okinawa, Japan during the war. When he was done telling me things I will never share with another living soul, he gave me a Japanese medallion that he had retrieved at the end of a lengthy punishing firefight. The medallion has Japanese writing on both sides with a depiction of a farm on it. Uncle Welbie told me to think about the medallion and the story that go's with it whenever life seems so rough you don't think you can face another day. I have never gotten to the point in my life that I ever wanted to give up. However, there have been times when life was beating me up and I was at a definite low. I would think about the story of the medallion and realize that my problems, though they seemed huge at the time, were small in the context of life. This would give me hope and make me think I could take on another day.

When I got older I found something better than the medallion that gives me hope, his name is Jesus Christ. Many people accuse me of using Jesus as a crutch and they would be right. He is the best crutch I have ever found. The same people that say I use Jesus as a crutch use alcohol, drugs, relationships, money, or social status as a crutch. Jesus has never let me down and I have leaned hard on him but the crutch has never broken. I can't say the same for alcohol and drugs, because as soon as the affect from the substance is out of a persons system there is still that emptiness inside them that can only be filled with God. Relationships are fulfilling until the person you have the relationship with turns on you and hurt you. Money and social status can bring material happiness but cannot fill that void you feel when you are all alone. When you die and stand before God, your money and material possessions will not impress him. God made the entire world and is not awed by money and possessions; he cares only about your relationship with him. How much time did you spend getting to know God?

In 1924, William Dale Houghton was born in Detroit, Michigan. He was the fourth boy and fifth child. William was called Bill, as William was my father.

Blanche Elaine Houghton was born in 1928 in Detroit, Michigan. She was the youngest girl of the family and sixth child. Blanche, not to be outdone by her older brothers, went by her middle name, Elaine. Elaine married Richard Wood in 1946. They had five children: Roxanne, Cathy, Richard Jr., Timothy, and Jeffrey. They built a home not far from the Houghton farm and lived there all their child-rearing years.

Kenneth Scott Houghton (known as Scott) was born, the last of seven children, on August 27, 1935. There were twenty years between him and Eleanor, his older sister. He lived his entire life within a five-mile radius, and he farmed and did carpentry just like his father. He married Donna Lieter in August of 1954. After getting married, he lived on the Houghton farm for a few years before building a home on the north end of his father's farm. Donna and Scott had four children, and all their names started with a K: Katie, Kelly, Kenneth Jr., and Karrie. Scott died on September 20, 1994 from polycystic kidney disease. I had the honor of being a pallbearer at his funeral.

Kenneth Scott Houghton

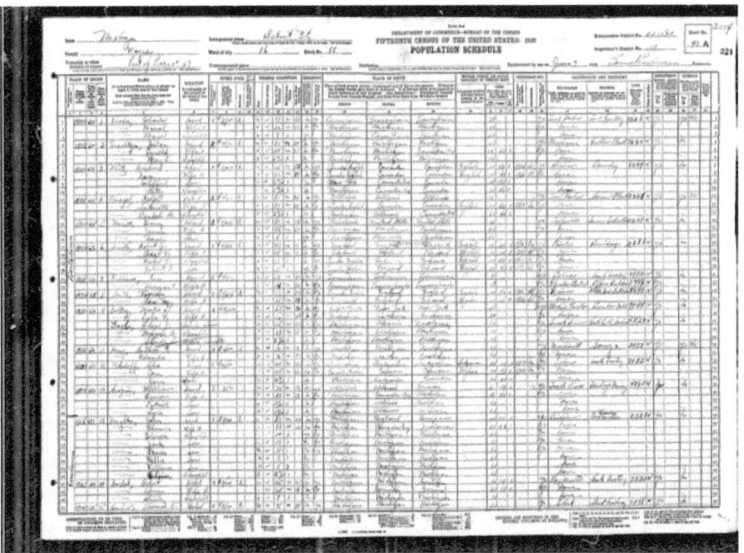

1930 Federal Census – Donald, Blanche, Eleanor, Jack, Lee, Welbie, William, Elaine. Detroit, Michigan.

In 1927, the Houghton family bought their first radio. They were living in Detroit and could get excellent reception. The broadcast hours were irregular and some stations were only on for four or five hours a day. Some of their favorite radio programs were the *Amos 'n Andy* comedy show, *The Detective Story Hour* starring the Shadow, *Fibber McGee and Molly*, *The Lone Ranger*, and *The Mercury Theater On the Air* with  Orson Wells. As the children got older, they would hurry home to listen to their favorite radio programs.

At the age of three, William could not figure out how all those people got into that little box. He heard the voices coming from the radio and thought they somehow lived in there.

In 1934, my father went to see a Detroit Tigers baseball game at Navin Field with his father. He was nine years old and a fan that year because the Tigers were on fire. The Tigers finished first in the American League and played in the World Series against St. Louis. My father rode a city bus to the game, which cost five cents per person. At this time in Detroit's history, it was still safe to walk the streets and ride the bus.

Dad watched number 5, Hank Greenburg, and number 2, Charlie Gehringer, both hit homeruns that day. Schoolboy Rowe was the pitcher, pitched the entire game, and got the win. The ticket to the game was fifty cents, and the experience was priceless. The cost of a bleacher seat to see the World Series that year at Navin Field was one dollar with ten cents' worth of tax.

The Houghton farm

The Houghton Farm

Mt Pleasant, Michigan
1935 - 1972

In June of 1935 during the Great Depression, John III and Blanche would move the family back to the Mt. Pleasant area near the Chippewa River on South Gilmore Road. The Depression had its stranglehold on the country and John III's contracting business could no longer withstand its death grip. My dad remembers the day his father loaded the last of their possessions into the family car and they moved to Mt. Pleasant.

They built a home near the Chippewa River and started farming to ride out the Depression. The first home was a temporary structure used to house the family until a more permanent home could be built near highway M20. The rain always managed to find the holes in the roof, while in the winter the icy winds never failed to blow through the cracks in the walls. William told stories of waking up in the morning during the winter and shaking the snow that had blown in through the cracks in the walls from his bedcovers. During the winter, the children would walk on the frozen river to their one-room schoolhouse. The school held grades K-8, and after eighth grade, they had to find rides into Mt. Pleasant for high school.

They had an ice shed in which they kept blocks of ice that they cut from the river during the winter. The ice was kept under layers of wood shavings and used in the small family icebox throughout the summer. During the winter months they had a natural icebox they used called the State of Michigan.

Christmas was an austere time during the Depression for most families. If you went to bed at night with a full stomach, it had been a good day. The children remember what gifts were like at Christmastime when there was barely enough money to put food on the table. In the tough years of the Depression, they would receive a small paper bag filled with an orange, an apple, a banana, some nuts, and some hard candy. My dad says that one Christmas the money was so tight that Grandma had to cut the pockets out of the boy's pants just so they had something to play with. He heard that joke during the Depression and would tell it when anyone started telling stories about the hard times they went through.

John III bought another eighty acres on Gilmore road near highway M20 and built three homes, a barn, and several outbuildings. The farm had various animals, including hogs, cattle, chickens and turkeys. All the children had chores on the farm whilst growing up, and one responsibility William had was killing and cleaning the chicken for supper. He disliked this job immensely. He never got the memory or smells associated with this task out of his mind and consequently there were very few chicken meals at my house when I was growing up.

For an adventure, William and his close friend William Millard hitchhiked to Niagara Falls, Canada when they were both sixteen years old. They camped under billboards and lived on the generosity of motorist along the way. Hitchhiking was common and relatively safe in the thirties and forties. They spent several nights on the road before they came back home. In just a few short months, William would join the Marines.

Welbie, Bill Millard, and William Houghton, 1941.

Welbie, second row, first on left. William, top row, last on right.

A World at War

1941-1945

On December 7, 1941, Japan attacked the United States naval fleet anchored at Pearl Harbor, Hawaii. This attack launched the United States into World War II, and the Houghton boys, as well as all American boys at the time, started talking about enlisting in the service to fight the Japanese.

The first of the boys to enlist was Lee (called Maurice) in February 1942. Welbie and William were both itching to get into the service and wanted to go together. William was only seventeen and would need his parents' permission to go. William and Welbie worked on their parents to persuade them that they should let William enlist. Finally, after much persuasion, their parents gave their consent, and William and Welbie enlisted on March 24, 1942. Last to go was John IV (called Jack), the oldest of the boys to serve. They all became "leathernecks," a term used for all Marines.

William and Welbie went to boot camp together and spent the first two years of the war together in San Diego, California; Honolulu, Hawaii; and the Midway Islands. Boot camp was challenging for both William and Welbie, but they had one another to depend on. They both liked the variety of foods served at the mess hall and often swapped foods with each other. Welbie liked

Welbie   **William**

sweets, and William liked meat and potatoes. William always gave his older brother his desserts in exchange for his meat or potatoes.

In March 1944, Welbie and William were separated. William was sent to Panama to guard prisoners of war and the Panama Canal, and Welbie was sent to Camp Pendleton and then to Guam to begin training for the invasion of Okinawa, Japan. During his time at Panama, William began to save all his wartime correspondence with friends and family.

William, Welbie, and Lee Houghton.

Letters

In the not-too-distant past, before the common use of telephones and before cell phones and e-mail, people used to write down their thoughts, feelings, and daily activities on a piece of paper. The paper was then folded and placed in an envelope that was addressed, stamped, and carried to the post office. They called that paper "a letter" and it would take days or weeks for that letter to get to its recipient, who was addressed on the envelope.

Some people lived for that time of day when the mail carrier would bring the mail. During the war years, a letter from home made or broke a soldier's day. Reading the letter was a way of escaping the hell they were in and reconnecting with life back home. The letter would be read and reread several times until the next one came. My father, William Houghton, kept a good portion of his wartime correspondence from family, including his brothers who wrote to him.

March 14 to May 23, 1944

San Diego, California – Camp Elliot
to New River, North Carolina – Camp Lejuene

William went stateside to San Diego, California and was stationed at Camp Elliot from March 14, 1944 to May 1944, when he was transferred to Camp Lejuene at New River, North Carolina. His travel expenses for the travel from the Pacific Ocean to the Atlantic Ocean were eighty-two dollars and two cents, and he was paid twelve dollars for food. William was now nineteen years old and this was the first time he would be alone—Welbie would stay in California at Camp Pendleton.

While William was traveling on the train from San Diego, he got a piece of coal ash in his eye from the train engine. He suffered from the speck of ash all day until an elderly man on the train showed him how to pull his eyelid out and down and roll his eye. He tried it and it worked; the intruder was now gone. My dad taught me that trick while sharing the story with me when I was ten years old.

After a short stay at Camp Lejuene, William boarded a ship and went to Panama. Welbie was sent to the Fourth Marines, Second

Battalion Company E, stationed in Guam, to begin training for the invasion of Okinawa, Japan. Welbie would now be with his older brother Lee, who was also in the Fourth Marines, Third Battalion Company L. William's third brother, Jack, also participated in the battle at Okinawa with the Fifth Marines.

The letters begin in November of 1944. All letters were censored by the military before mailing, and at times the boys were not allowed to say where they were, so they just would give hints to their location instead.

#

November 6, 1944
Dear Bill,

Well how's everything with you. We are somewhere in the South Pacific. We crossed the dateline and equator on our way. You know what you missed the first time out with Welbie. Welbie and I saw Jack at Camp Pendleton before he left. He left a month before we did. I do not know where he is. Welbie and I are still together. He is in one battalion and I am in another battalion but same regiment.

Love **Maurice (Lee)**

#

November 6, 1944
Dear Bill,

Maurice and I are together. I always manage to be with one of you. I guess I am lucky that way. I got married to Betty and if you get a chance to write her she lives at 704 N. Cayuga St. Ithaca New York. Mom and Elaine were at the wedding. Jack left a month before we did. Do you know where he is? Have to go.

Your brother **Welbie**

#

Welbie and Lee were stationed at Guam, training for the largest invasion the world has ever seen: Okinawa, Japan. The invasion would consist of 1,439 ships and over 60,000 soldiers with 120,000 men in reserve.

#

December 25, 1944

Christmas card from Welbie:

May he who was born

When the world was at peace,

Grant his peace to all men in a world at war.

Dear Bill,

This is our first Christmas apart. Looking forward to the day when this war is over and all of us can be together again. Bill, have a nice Christmas.

Welbie

#

December 27, 1944

Hello Bill,

It's the 27th of December and another Christmas has gone by. It was the same here as it was when we were together on Midway, remember? I guess I'm lucky, the last two I spent with you and this one with Maurice. Maurice had guard duty today. We don't have to pull guard duty often. Betty writes me nearly every day. Did you get the picture of her I sent you? Isn't she swell? I don't know how I could have done better. When you get to the States look her up Bill. Jack was supposed to come over but he couldn't because he is in sickbay. Maurice and I are going to try to get over to see him for New Year's. I got a letter from Mom and Elaine with Scottie's picture in it. Boy they are growing up away from us. Good luck

Your brother **Welbie**

#

December 31, 1944
Dear Bill,

I see Welbie every night. He lives about a quarter mile from me. Jack is on an island about 60 miles away. We plan to see him soon. What did you do for Christmas? Doesn't seem like Christmas or even winter here, more like July back home.

Love your brother **Maurice**

#

February 23, 1945
Dear Bill,

Got your letter last night and was sure glad to hear from you. I wrote you about four months ago, did you get the letter? I lost your address. Yes, Bill I saw Maurice and Welbie, we had a good time together, as good as you can have here. Well Bill I am on mess duty for the first time cannot say as I like it much. I sent home a nip rifle for dad yesterday. Bill how did you know where I was? Did you know where the 1st division was? Maurice and Welbie are together, I wish you and I could be together, but I am glad you are in Panama. Where we are going is not going to be pleasant.

Love your brother **Jack**
Co. L 1st Battalion 5th Marine Division

\#

April 3, 1945

Dear Son,

We received your letter and were glad to hear from you. You are an uncle again, it's a girl. Betty had her baby and it was a little soon. It weighed 4lbs and 4oz. We received a telegram from Betty's mother. My heart sank when the telegram first came, you know how everyone hates receiving telegrams these days, but it was good news. We don't know what they named her yet.

Lots of love as ever. Mom

\#

May 12, 1945

Hello Bill,

Jack and I are on Okinawa. Maurice got sick aboard the ship the day before we landed and was sent to Guam. I haven't heard from him have you? The other day Jack came over to see me, was I surprised. He looks as good as ever I seen him. The women here are dirty and the places they live in are like the pigs shacks back home. Huts with straw roofs, they don't have beds or chairs just a mat to sleep on. They cook like back in the Stone Age and because they eat with chopsticks, they are awful small. When they walk, they got more of a chop chop step to it. They bow to you and grin at you. That is the dark side of Okinawan people, of course in peacetime it would be a lot different.

Love your brother Welbie

William and Welbie.

Operation Iceberg

Okinawa, Japan
April to July 1945

The assault on Okinawa was called Operation Iceberg and began on April 1, 1945—April Fool's Day and Easter Sunday—at 0830. The Fourth Marines would lead the assault on the shore. Eighty percent casualties were expected for the initial wave of troops involved in taking the beach. The Fourth Marines, among the first wave of soldiers to hit the beach, were surprised because there was no shooting; little did they know that the Japanese had decided not to defend the beach and had already dug themselves in to the caves and tunnels in the mountains. The Japanese knew they could not win the battle, and their mission was to make the Americans pay a heavy price to take Okinawa. Their goal was to kill ten Americans for every Japanese life taken on the island.

Welbie and Lee's Fourth Marines were on the island all eighty-two days of the battle. Their major battles were at Mount Yaetake, Naha, Sugarloaf Hill, and the assault on Oruku Peninsula. The Fourth Marines alone would suffer 110% losses, a figure that reflects both adding replacements and their high attrition rate after joining. One company of the Fourth Marines (Company E, Welbie's company) would suffer the loss of sixty-five men and three consecutive company commanders on April 15 while trying to take Mount Yaetake. I would like to concentrate on one battle Welbie and Lee were involved in, Hell's own cesspool, Sugarloaf Hill. I will detail only Welbie's 2/4 E Company and Lee's 3/4 L Company. All details of the battle are from firsthand sources.

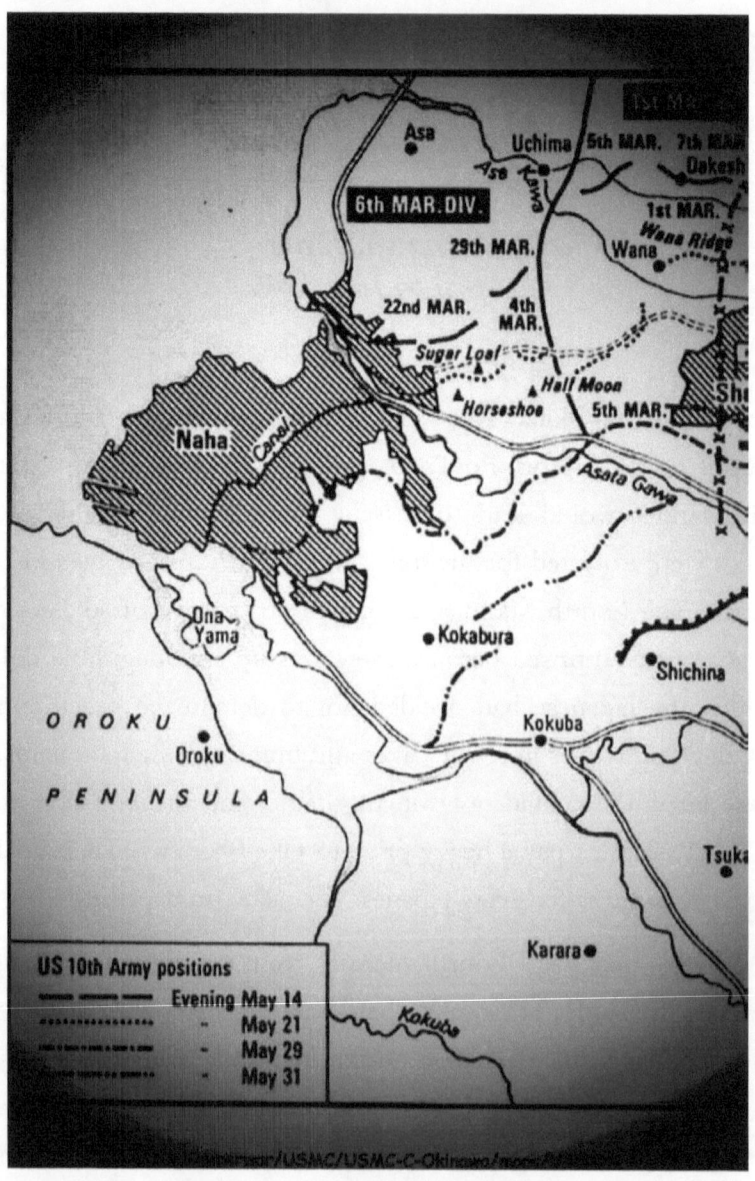

Sugarloaf Hill

May 1945

The battle to take Sugarloaf Hill had been going on for several days with the Twenty-Ninth Marines doing the fighting. The Twenty-Ninth had been ripped to pieces by the Japanese and could not advance any further. On May 18, General Geiger released the Fourth Marines from corps reserve. On the early morning of May 19, 2/4 and 3/4 moved out in the approach march to relieve the assault battalions of the Twenty-Ninth, which were already in place.

Harassing mortar and artillery fire falling on the relieving columns hampered their movements, but by 1430, 2/4 was in place on the left, 3/4 on the right, and the Twenty-Ninth had displaced to the rear. The relief effort cost the Fourth Marines over seventy casualties.

The Japanese, who had observed the relief, immediately launched a counterattack against Welbie's 2/4, which was in an exposed position near Half Moon Hill. A sharp firefight erupted for about two hours, and then the Japanese broke contact and retired. Following the well-placed fire of artillery and mortars, Welbie's 2/4 and Lee's 3/4 moved out in the assault on May 20. Both battalions were supported by tanks and made rapid progress for about two hundred yards when they were brought to a halt by a torrent of enemy fire. The Japanese, who were deeply entrenched on Half Moon Hill and Horseshoe Hill, suddenly met the advance with a hail of small arms, machinegun, and artillery and mortar fire. The enemy's artillery observers on Shuri Ridge were virtually looking down the Marines' throats and could easily control and direct very accurate fire from their hidden gun positions. Consequently, they were able to inflict heavy casualties on the assaulting line.

At about 1000 hours, Welbie's Company E was ordered to assault and flank the Japanese on the left. Company E's advance was slow, due in part to the enemy fire that was coming from three directions and the open ground they had to traverse. Despite heavy casualties and the volume of mortar fire, they reached the forward slope of their objective and dug in for the night. Although 2/4's position was unusually close to that of the Japanese, they gained vital ground and held secure positions.

On the right, Lee's battalion, 3/4, pressed their assault against a network of supporting emplacements in the caves along the forward slope of Horseshoe Ridge. Using demolitions, flamethrowers, and the direct fire of the supporting tanks, Lee's company L methodically reduced the enemy's line of defense. They suffered heavy casualties, but by 1600, when the attack was halted, they were on the battalion's objective. The Third Battalion then dug in for the night.

Quiet prevailed along the Marines' lines in the early hours of darkness. Only the usual but constant harassing artillery and mortar fire interrupted the calm. Around 2200 the volume of fire suddenly increased, and bursts of white phosphorous and colored smoke signaled the launching of the expected counterattack. A force of over seven hundred battle-tested enemy troops hit the front of L Company with a furious assault.

The response of the Third Battalion and all their supports was instantaneous and greatly destructive. The pre-registered concentrations of six artillery battalions crashed down on the attacking force and naval guns brightened the sky over the entire area. The 60mm mortars of each company and the battalion's 81mm's quickly laid fire on their registered zones. This was just the beginning, before the assault was crushed, fifteen battalions of artillery would be firing on the Third Battalion front and all avenues of approach.

The Japanese, who realized there was a limit to how close artillery and mortars would be used in front of our own lines, closed up to the Marines' positions. The ensuing battle was close in, vicious, savage, and at times hand-to-hand. The battle had to be won at close range with grenades, machineguns, other small arms, and the knife and bayonet.

By one in the morning, the issue had been resolved. The few Japanese who had penetrated the lines were quickly killed and mopping up of the area was in progress. The wounded were attended to and evacuated, but the removal of the dead would have to wait until morning.

With the rising of the sun on the morning of the 21st, the grisly results of the night before were revealed. In front of Lee's company lines lay over five hundred dead Japanese. Heavy rains would start on the night of the 22nd, making the entire area of operations a sea of mud. There were so many dead bodies strung about that when someone lost their footing in the slippery mud and slid down the hill, by the time they reached the bottom their fatigue pockets would be full of maggots from the rotting bodies strewn on the hill. The stench from the decaying bodies was unbearable.

The battle for Sugarloaf Hill would continue another eight days before the Japanese finally retreated during the night. More American soldiers would be killed per square foot at Sugarloaf—over three thousand—than in any other battle in the entire four years of the war.

Sugarloaf was now taken and it was only the end of May. The boys had another month and a half of fighting to go.

#

July 1945

Letter written on Red Cross stationery

Hello Bill,

Well Bill I got in the way of a little shrapnel, a piece in the hand, and another in the arm. But you can see from the way I am writing it is not so bad so don't worry. They will take it out in a couple days. I do not know how straight this is but one of the guys that knows Maurice said he got it in the arm too. Not bad so do not worry. I have not heard from Jack yet, but will write as soon as I hear from him. I sure hope he made out as good as we did. The light is going out so I will have to stop for now.

Your brother **Welbie**

HOFFMAN, John Vincent, Pfc., USMCR. Parents, Mr. and Mrs. John Hoffman, 328 Logan Ave., New York City.

HOFFMAN, Julius Romanoff, Lieutenant (jg), USNR. Wife, Mrs. Alice Eleanor Hoffman, 1429 Dean St., Schenectady.

HOFFMAN, Emil J., Pvt., USMCR. Mother, Mrs. Caroline H. Hoffman, 364 Longnecker St., Buffalo.

HOFHEINZ, Peter Stanley, Baker 3c, USNR. Parents, Mr. and Mrs. Eugene Hofheinz, 345 Bleecker St., Brooklyn.

HOGAN, Joseph, Chief Cook, USN. Wife, Mrs. Mary Estelle Hogan, 580 Nicholas Ave., New York.

HOLBROOK, Gustave P., Pfc., USMCR. Sister, Miss Elizabeth Holbrook, 17623 137th Ave., Springfield Gardens.

HOLDEN, Douglas E., Pfc., USMC. Parents, Mr. and Mrs. Ray F. Holden, Rt. 2, Union.

HOLDEN, George B., Pfc., USMCR. Father, Col. Charles A. Holden, 230 Park Ave., New York.

HOLDEN, William A., Pvt., USMCR. Parents, Mr. and Mrs. James Holden, 517 W. 134th St., New York.

HOLDER, Horace Dinsmore, Cook 3c, USMCR. Mother, Mrs. Inez Giddens, 301 W. 130th St., New York.

HOLLAND, George F., Pvt., USMCR. Parents, Mr. and Mrs. Patrick F. Holland, 454 Wildwood Ave., Salamanca.

HOLLAND, George Robert, Seaman 2c, USN. Father, Mr. James A. Holland, Rt. 1, Narrowsburg.

HOLLAR, Turner Oliver, Jr., Pfc., USMCR. Wife, Mrs. Jean C. Hollar, 47-34 188th St., Flushing.

HOLLENBECK, William F., Sgt., USMCR. Mother, Mrs. Marjorie Hollenbeck, 188 Bronxville Rd., Bronxville.

HOLLENBECK, Willis E., Cpl., USMCR. Mother, Mrs. Irene H. Cochrane, Star Rt., Phoenix.

HOLLERAN, Edward J., Pfc., USMCR. Wife, Mrs. Mary E Holleran, 614½ 21st St., Niagara Falls.

HOLMES, Charles H., Pvt., USMCR. Parents, Mr. and Mrs. Fred G. Holmes, 311 9th St., Niagara Falls.

HOLMES, Charles Henry, Seaman 2c, USNR. Mother, Mrs. Mae Isabell Holmes, 1039 Olmstead Ave., Bronx, New York.

HOLMES, Charles R., Pfc., USMCR. Parents, Mr. and Mrs. Raymond Holmes, 1641 Miller St., Utica.

HOLMES, Clifford A., Gunnery Sgt., USMC. Wife, Mrs. Clifford A. Holmes, 4019 Ithaca St., Elmhurst, Flushing.

HOLMES, Herbert Underwood, Gunner's Mate 1c, USNR. Wife, Mrs. Elsie Anna Holmes, 1831 Summerfield Ave., Bridgwood, Brooklyn.

HOLMES, James Wilkinson, Pay Clerk, Supply Corps, USNR. Wife, Mrs. Bertha Schaadt Holmes, Guilderland.

HOLMQUIST, Carl Eric, Chief Machinist's Mate, USN. Mother, Mrs. Caroline Holmquist, 30 Monument Ave., Glen Falls.

HOLMSTROM, Wilbur Emil, Pfc., USMC. Wife, Mrs. Lenore R. Holmstrom, Box 503, Millbrook.

HOLOCINSKI, William E., Cpl., USMC. Parents, Mr. and Mrs. Joseph Holocinski, 27 Palmer St., Gowanda.

HOLODNIAK, Walter, Aviation Ordnanceman 2c, USNR. Mother, Mrs. Anna Holodniak, 218 E. 5th St., New York.

HOLOHAN, John David, Pharmacist's Mate 2c, USNR. Parents, Mr. and Mrs. Frank Charles Holohan, Boght Corners, Cohoes.

HOLSAPPLE, Penn H., 1st Lieutenant, USMCR. Wife, Mrs. Barbara J. Holsapple, 152 Brewster Rd., Scarsdale.

HOLSTEN, Joseph Henry, Pharmacist's Mate 3c, USNR. Parents, Mr. and Mrs. Joseph Holsten, W. 2d St., Ronkonkoma.

HOLTZCLAW, William Merideth, Lieutenant, Supply Corps, USNR. Wife, Mrs. Marion Eugenia Holtzclaw, 145 Parkwood Ave., Kenmore, Buffalo.

HOLZER, Edward F., Pfc., USMC. Mother, Mrs. Mary Holzer, 21-65-42 St., Astoria, Long Island City.

HOLZHAUSER, Warren Fred, Pfc., USMCR. Wife, Mrs. Barbara Holzhauser, 64 N. William St., Baldwin.

HOMA, George J., Jr., Pfc., USMCR. Father, Mr. George J. Homa, Sr., 327 Rogers Ave., Endicott.

HOMA, Paul, Cpl., USMCR. Halfbrother, Mr. Michael Gramata, 250 Oak St., Binghamton.

HONIS, Donald James, Pvt., USMC. Parents, Mr. and Mrs. Joseph Honis, 7½ Cayuga St., Syracuse.

HONKANEN, Veikko Victor, Pvt., USMCR. Sister, Mrs. Helvi Novall, 648 47th St., Brooklyn.

HOOD, James V., Sgt., USMCR. Parents, Mr. and Mrs. James Hood, 240-23 144th Ave., Rosedale.

HOOD, Richard William, Cpl., USMCR. Mother, Mrs. Frieda Hood, 461 Fairview Ave., Ridgewood, Brooklyn.

HOOK, Andrew H., Pfc., USMCR. Parents, Mr. and Mrs. Michael Hook, 97 Avenue D, New York.

HOOK, Peter, Pfc., USMCR. Mother, Mrs. Anna Hook, 123 Washington St., Utica.

HOOPES, Warrick G., Captain, USMCR. Wife, Mrs. Warrick G. Hoopes, Hudson View Gardens, 183d and Pinehurst Ave., New York.

HOOPS, John Thomas, Yeoman 1c, USN. Parents, Mr. and Mrs. John Herman Hoops, 62-40 80th Rd., Glendale, Brooklyn.

HOOSE, Eugene W., Pvt., USMCR. Father, Mr. Eugene Hoose, 25 Gregory St., Gloversville.

HOPFER, Albert Vincent, Cpl., USMCR. Parents, Mr. and Mrs. George Hopfer, 5 Whipple St., Brooklyn.

HOPFER, Arthur Otto, Sgt., USMC. Parents, Mr. and Mrs. George Hopfer, 720 Flushing Ave., Brooklyn.

HOPKINS, Carlton J., Field Musician 1c, USMCR. Parents, Mr. and Mrs. Howard F. Hopkins, 128 Milton Ave, Ballston Spa.

HOPKINS, John J., Cpl., USMCR. Father, Mr. Thomas E. Hopkins, 377 8th St., Brooklyn.

HOPKINS, Lionel J., Pfc., USMCR. Mother, Mrs. Catherine F. Hopkins, 905 Belmont Ave., Utica.

HOPKINS, Robert Leonard, Pfc., USMCR. Parents, Mr. and Mrs. Jean W. Hopkins, 233 60th St., Brooklyn.

HORAN, James, Pfc., USMCR. Mother, Mrs. Alice Horan, 1616 8th Ave., Brooklyn.

HORCH, Wilbert W., Pvt., USMCR. Sister, Mrs. Alice J Farrington, 351 LeRoy Ave., Buffalo.

HORGAN, Cornelius J., Pfc., USMCR. Sister, Miss Kirby Horgan, 538 58th St., Brooklyn

HORNE, William R., Pvt., USMCR. Father, Mr. John R. Horne, 65 Broadway, New York.

HORNUNG, Harvey A., Cpl., USMCR. Parents, Mr. and Mrs. Ferdinand Hornung, 756 LaSalle Ave., Buffalo.

HORNUNG, William J., Pvt., USMCR. Parents, Mr. and Mrs. William C. Hornung, 839 Glenwood Ave., Buffalo.

HOROWITZ, Irving, Pfc., USMCR. Parents, Mr. and Mrs. Samuel Horowitz, 102 Liberty Ave., Brooklyn.

HORTON, Merle L., Cpl., USMCR. Father, Mr. Lewis Horton, 22 Willink St., Buffalo.

HORTON, Raymond A., Pfc., USMCR. Parents, Mr. and Mrs. Austin Horton, 65 Cayuga St., Homer.

HORTSCH, Arthur M., Pvt., USMC. Father, Mr. Charles A. Hortsch, 10 Bank St., Port Washington.

HOUDEK, William Peter, Seaman 1c, USNR. Parents, Mr. and Mrs. John Houdek, 70 Sumner Ave., Brooklyn.

HOUGHTALING, Elmond, Jr., Pfc., USMCR. Parents, Mr. and Mrs. Elmond Houghtaling, Sr., 33 Walnut St., Poughkeepsie.

HOUGHTON, Patrick, Aviation Machinist's Mate 2c, USNR. Parents, Mr. and Mrs. Patrick Houghton, 333 Ave. A, New York.

HOUGHTON, Welbie Elton, Cpl., USMC. Wife, Mrs. Betty J. Houghton, 704 N. Cayuga St. Ithaca.

HOUSEMAN, Lyell W., Cpl., USMCR. Parents, Mr. and Mrs. Franklin Houseman, Rt. 1, Lyndonville.

HOVEY, James D., Pfc., USMCR. Sister, Mrs. Earl Hastings, 91 Saratoga Ave., Ballston Spa.

HOWARD, Frank Jesse, Cpl., USMCR. Father, Mr. Frank Howard, 1337 E. 27th St., Brooklyn.

HOWARD, John W., Sgt., USMCR. Mother, Mrs. Chase Owen Howard, Hoffmans.

HOWARD, Robert Raymond, Watertender 1c, USN. Wife, Mrs. Elsie Gertrude Howard, 1714 Madison, South Ridgewood, Brooklyn.

HOWARD, William V., Jr., Sgt., USMC. Parents, Mr. and Mrs. William V. Howard, Sr, 429 Wellington Rd., Mineola.

HOWE, John J., Pfc., USMC. Parents, Mr. and Mrs. David J. Howe, 93 W. Lincoln Pl., Freeport.

Welbie Elton Houghton Cpl USMC, wounded in action announcement, 1945.

HOLLENBECK, Clifford Myron, Gunners' Mate 1c, USN. Wife, Mrs. Ellen Hollenbeck, 8120 Main St., Dexter.

HOLLOWAY, Harry N., Pfc., USMC. Mother, Mrs. Anna Holloway, 7401 Esper Blvd., Dearborn.

HOLM, Peter Leslie, Jr., Seaman 1c, USNR. Parents, Mr. and Mrs. Peter Holm, 613 Division St., Marquette.

HOLMAN, Jep, Chief Machinist, USN. Wife, Mrs. Adah Winsome Holman, 1850 Corunna Ave., Owosso.

HOLMES, Harry C., Pfc., USMC. Mother, Mrs. Nellie Holmes, Cedar Springs.

HOLMES, John W., Pfc., USMCR. Parents, Mr. and Mrs. Elwyn R. Holmes, 880 S. Joseph St., South Haven.

HOLOWEZKI, Walter J., Cpl., USMC. Father, Mr. Michael Holowezki, 15375 Freeland St., Detroit.

HOLSTINE, John Raymond, Cpl., USMCR. Parents, Mr. and Mrs. Glenn Holstine, 1509 W. Dartmouth St., Flint.

HOLSTROM, Harold Basil, Aviation Electrician's Mate 2c, USNR. Parents, Mr. and Mrs. Harry Joseph Holstrom, Sr., 1093 W. Southern Ave., Muskegon.

HOLTBY, Richard Wayne, Seaman 1c, USNR. Parents, Mr. and Mrs. Howard K. Holtby, 9739 McKinney Ave., Detroit.

HOLZMAN, Arnold Nicholas, Pfc., USMCR. Father, Mr. Nicholas Holzman, 11 Highland Towers, Detroit.

HOMIC, Stanley Robert, Pfc., USMC. Mother, Mrs. Catherine Homic, 3036 Trowbridge St., Hamtramck, Detroit.

HONKALA, George Matt, Pvt., USMCR. Wife, Mrs. Marion Honkala, 606 Yale Ave., Bessemer.

HOOPS, Carl Leslie, Machinist's Mate 1c, USNR. Wife, Mrs. Myrtle Ann Hoops, 1016 N. Maple St., Royal Oak.

HOPKINS, Jack Calten, Pvt., USMCR. Father, Mr. Freece B. Hopkins, 12845 Mohart Rd., Britton.

HOPKINS, James A., Pfc., USMCR. Mother, Mrs. Grace L. Hopkins, 647 E. 8th St., Traverse City.

HOPKINS, Lewis Uberto, Aviation Metalsmith 2c, USN. Parents, Mr. and Mrs. Oscar Whipple Hopkins, 3328 E. Michigan Ave., Lansing.

HOPPS, Edward N., Pfc., USMCR. Mother, Mrs. Bessie Hartt Hopps, 18885 Lancashire Rd., Detroit.

HORN, Roy Ellisworth, Seaman 2c, USNR. Parents, Mr. and Mrs. Henry Ellisworth Horn, 419 Michigan Ave., Detroit.

HORNEY, Allen Andrew, Ensign, USNR. Parents, Mr. and Mrs. Norman Horney, Box 65, Coloma.

HOROWITZ, Samuel, Machinist's Mate 3c, USNR. Wife, Mrs. June Horowitz, 1125 Lake Dr., Grand Rapids.

HORSLEY, Melvin C., Sgt., USMCR. Mother, Mrs. Jessie H. Wilcox, 49 Mechanic St., Pontiac.

HORTON, Thomas L., Pfc., USMCR. Father, Mr. George D. Horton, 23600 Buckingham St., Dearborn.

HORVATH, Colman J., Pfc., USMCR. Wife, Mrs. Esther B. Horvath, 600 S. Schroeder St., Detroit.

HOSTMAN, Joseph John, Fireman 1c, USNR. Father, Mr. John Hostman, 1215 Oak, Wyandotte.

HOUCK, James J., Pfc., USMC. Father, Mr. Frank Houck, 118 Waterford St., Pontiac.

HOUCK, LeRoy Price, Lieutenant (jg), USNR. Parents, Mr. and Mrs. John Rush Houck, 14488 Rochelle Ave., Detroit.

HOUGHTON, Floyd M., Sgt., USMC. Mother, Mrs. Veda I. Houghton, 110 S. 1st St., Manistique.

HOUGHTON, Lee Maurice, Pfc., USMC. Parents, Mr. and Mrs. John D. Houghton, RFD 2, Mt. Pleasant.

HOURAN, Francis C., Cpl., USMCR. Wife, Mrs. Francis C. Houran, 133 Orchard St., Chelsea.

HOUTZ, Ralph E., Pfc., USMC. Father, Mr. George E. Houtz, 20010 Farmington Rd., Farmington.

HOWARD, Denton D., Cpl., USMCR. Mother, Mrs. Sarah S. Smith, 812 E. Hamilton St., Flint.

HOWARD, George E., Pvt., USMCR. Wife, Mrs. George E. Howard, 3602 Branch Rd., Flint.

HOWARTH, Donald L., Pfc., USMC. Mother, Mrs. Julie L. Moss, 10628 Peerless Ave., Detroit.

HOWAT, William, Jr., Seaman 2c, USN. Mother, Mrs. Antoinette Recker, 3587 Gladwin, Detroit.

HOWELL, Irving Arthur, Aviation Ordnanceman 3c, USNR. Parents, Mr. and Mrs. Arthur J. Howell, 844 Franklin St., SE, Grand Rapids.

HOWLE, Marvin R., Pfc., USMCR. Mother, Mrs. Helen Famularo, 13832 Young St., Detroit.

HOYDIC, Robert C., Pvt., USMCR. Mother, Mrs. Jennie Hoydic, 6458 Maxwell St., Detroit.

HOYT, Loren T., Cpl., USMCR. Wife, Mrs. Loren T. Hoyt, 626 Monroe St., Mt. Morris.

HUBBARD, Calvin Ernest, Pfc., USMCR. Wife, Mrs. Dorothy M. Hubbard, 1937 Delaware Ave., Detroit.

HUBBARD, Eugene W., Pvt., USMCR. Parents, Mr. and Mrs. Louis T. Hubbard, 4128 Pelham Rd., Dearborn.

HUBBARD, Hollway, Fireman 1c, USNR. Father, Mr. William H. Hubbard, 425 W. Iroquois, Pontiac.

HUBBARD, Thomas Henry, Jr., Patternmaker 1c, USN. Father, Mr. Thomas Henry Hubbard, Sr., Whitehall.

HUBBARD, Walter M., Pfc., USMCR. Parents, Mr. and Mrs. Harry Hubbard, 1155 E. Forest St., Ypsilanti.

HUBBARD, Willard Wright, Lieutenant (jg), USNR. Wife, Mrs. Sara R. Hubbard, 625 Windsor Ter., Grand Rapids.

HUDSON, Clyde Thomas, Seaman 1c, USNR. Parents, Mr. and Mrs. Clyde Euclid Hudson, 721 Alexander St., SE, Grand Rapids.

HUDSON, Richard A., Pvt., USMCR. Parents, Mr. and Mrs. Albert J. Hudson, Rt. 2, Cheboygan.

HUEY, Paul E., Pfc., USMCR. Father, Mr. Fred Huey, RFD 2, Freeland.

HUFFMAN, John M., 2d Lieutenant, USMCR. Wife, Mrs. John Miles Huffman, 640 E. Lewiston, Ferndale, Detroit.

HUGGINS, Sherwood B., Sgt., USMCR. Wife, Mrs. Sherwood B. Huggins, 8328 Leander St., Detroit.

HUGHES, Clarence, Jr., Pfc., USMCR. Mother, Mrs. Philomena H. Skogaland, 124 Conrad St., NE, Grand Rapids.

HUGHES, James Russell, Lieutenant, USNR. Wife, Mrs. Margaret W. Hughes, Standish.

HUGHSON, Robert James, Field Cook, USMCR. Parents, Mr. and Mrs. Samuel J. Hughson, 517 W. North St., Kalamazoo.

HULL, David Carl, Seaman 2c, USNR. Mother, Mrs. Tina Loveless, Rt. 2, Waxford Co., Cadillac.

HULL, Robert Edward, Watertender 2c, USN. Parents, Mr. and Mrs. Rueben Stephen Hull, 3815 Homewood Ave., Lansing.

HULTS, Allen Harold, Pfc., USMCR. Mother, Mrs. Marie W. Garms, 93 Inn Rd., Battle Creek.

HUNSAKER, Robert J., Pfc., USMCR. Mother, Mrs. Violet Morris, 20086 Inkster Rd., Detroit.

HURD, Edwin W., Pfc., USMCR. Parents, Mr. and Mrs. Edwin P. Hurd, 741 E. Grand Blvd., Detroit.

HURN, William Joseph, Sgt., USMC. Father, Mr. Dewey Hurn, 1406 Indiana, Flint.

HUSTED, Leon Jack, Technical Sgt., USMC. Wife, Mrs. Norma I. Husted, Rt. 1, Williamston.

HUTCHINS, Clayton J., Machinist's Mate 3c, USNR. Wife, Mrs. Eclose Hutchins, 1064 Hill Crest, Huron Gardens, Pontiac.

HUTCHINS, Robert Lloyd, Cpl., USMC. Parents, Mr. and Mrs. John H, Hutchins, 605 Baker St., Lansing.

HUTCHINSON, Richard Wright, Pfc., USMCR. Parents, Mr. and Mrs. Glenn W. Hutchinson, 4314 Grand Ave., Detroit.

HUTSON, Fay LeRoy, Seaman 1c, USNR. Wife, Mrs. Nina Hutson, Stanwood.

I

IBBOTSON, John A., Pfc., USMCR. Mother, Mrs. Nellie E. Ibbotson, 2050 Coolidge Dr., Flint.

IKENBURG, Edward James, Seaman 2c, USNR. Parents, Mr. and Mrs. Edward R. Ikenburg, 1732 Teel Ave., Lansing.

IMPELLIZZERI, Donald J., Pvt., USMCR. Parents, Mr. and Mrs. Samuel Impellizzeri, 5720 Fairview St., Detroit.

INGERSOLL, Norman Neil, Pvt., USMC. Parents, Mr. and Mrs. Claude Ingersoll, 467 Knapp St., Grand Rapids.

INMAN, Leon J., Pfc., USMCR. Mother, Mrs. Hazel Inman, Rose City.

IOVAN, Peter D., Pvt., USMCR. Parents, Mr. and Mrs. Damian Iovan, 111 Cottage Grove, Highland Park, Detroit.

Lee Maurice Houghton Pfc. USMC, wounded in action announcement, 1945.

#

July 1945
Letter written on Red Cross stationery

Dear Bill,

I received your letter and was damn glad to hear from you. Yes, I got sick the day before we hit Okinawa and was sent back to Guam. I had amoebic dysentery. I came back to Okinawa the middle of May. I saw Welbie once for about two minutes. We were moving up to the frontlines on Sugarloaf Hill and past his company. They moved up behind us. Boy there is a hotspot you probably heard about it nothing they say is bad enough. I saw Welbie again yesterday, he is OK. In a day or two, we are going to see how Jack made out. I have not seen him or heard from him since we hit this rock. Welbie saw him once before we moved to Southern Okinawa. While we where in Naha I caught a piece of shrapnel in the left arm. It is not bad, I was only in the hospital 15 days, and then back to duty. Welbie was hit in the hand and arm after I was. He is OK and back to duty. Well Bill I am glad you are where you are instead of here. I know that you have to put up with a lot of crap where you are from people who rank. Most of them birds can't take orders let alone give them. Take care of yourself.

Your brother **Maurice**

#

July 2, 1945

Dear Bill,

How is everything going with you? Everything is fine with me now that Okinawa is secured. It has been a long hard fight. Maurice, Welbie and I were all together yesterday and I sure was glad to see them, we are all OK now. Maurice and Welbie both were hit and were in the hospital. I was the lucky one and didn't get hit. I have not written you in a long time but you know you cannot write when you are fighting. Maurice, Welbie, and I had our picture made yesterday; one of the boys had a camera and took our picture. I will send you a copy.

With love your brother **Jack**

Welbie, Jack, and Lee. Okinawa, Japan July 2, 1945.

#

July 6, 1945

All three boys were together and sent three letters in the same envelope.

Dear Bill,

As I am writing this Welbie, Jack, and I are all together. It will probably be the last time for sometime. I sent home some souvenirs, nothing much a flag, rifle, and some money.

Take care your brother **Maurice**

#

Dear Bill,

Maurice, Welbie, and I are all together today. It sure is good to see them and know that they are all right. It will be a great day when all four of us are together again. Maurice and Welbie are writing in this letter so I will close for now.

Love your brother **Jack**

#

Hello Bill,

How is the boy? Maurice, Jack, and I are all together writing this letter. We are about to cook chow. We have to make it ourselves, you know just like camping. We had our picture made and sent you one. Boy do we look like hell, I think you will agree. Well Bill better stop for now.

Your brother **Welbie**

#

July 8, 1945

Dear brother Bill,

Well Bill how is the Marine Corp and you getting along? Are you OK? For a while there during the fighting I did not care what happened to me, but I am feeling OK now. I am sending you some nip money in the letter, 10 yen, it is the same as one U.S. dollar. I will not be seeing Welbie and Maurice for a long time, maybe not until the war is over. They are going to Guam and then some place very dangerous and bad. I am still on Okinawa and don't know how long I will be here.

Keep writing love **Jack**

#

The battle for Okinawa was decided in July and the Fourth Marines were redeployed to Guam to begin training for the invasion of mainland Japan. They were told the battle to take the islands of Japan could cost over one million American lives. Having just finished fighting at Okinawa, they knew that their prospects for survival were low because they would be the initial wave of soldiers to hit the island.

#

August 5, 1945

Bill,

Welbie and I are OK. We have not heard from Jack since we left Okinawa. I heard from Billy Millard and he is in the Philippines. He does not care for the fighting either. Well Bill even though you do not like it where you are at I am glad you are there. Three of us out here are enough. This fighting is no good. I don't mind the sniper fire so much, but those shells and mortars sure are hell on the moral. One of those eight-inch shells has a scream as if all hell is loose. When one lands next to your hole, it feels like someone took a club and hit you over the head and kicked you in the guts. I will be damn glad when this fighting is over.

Your brother **Maurice**

#

The atomic bombs dropped on Hiroshima and Nagasaki hastened Japan's decision to effect a complete capitulation on August 14, 1945. The war with Japan was finally over.

#

August 21, 1945
Dear Bill,

Well how do you feel now that the war is over? It sure makes me feel good. It will not be long before I see that daughter of mine. Jean said that Mary has the measles. Well Bill you will be out of the Corp before I will, I wish we could all get out and go home together, wouldn't that be a sight.

Love **Jack**

#

On August 15, the Fourth Marines were deployed to occupy Japan. The Fourth Marines were personally chosen by General Shepherd to be the first American unit to land on Japan. On August 30, 1945, the first unit ashore was Welbie's Second Battalion, landing at Futtsa Cape at 0600. They were the first foreign invaders ever to touch the Japanese mainland.

#

September 30, 1945
Bill,

The Marines are cutting back to a peacetime outfit. I hope they get rid of me. I have not seen Tokyo yet but hope to before I leave, it is only 40 miles away.

Maurice

#

2nd battalion 4th Marines landing at Futtsu Saki, Japan. August 30,1945
Photo from National Archives 127-N-134867

October 12, 1945
Dear Bill,

I have not written for some time and you will see later in this letter why. I am in Japan and it is a rotten place. The women look like pigs and are dirty. When we first came here August 30, we did not have liberty for five days. We were on patrols to feel the people out. The first few patrols we went on there was no one around. They all took off to the hills. They had been told the Americans would kill them. After a few days, they started coming back. We are at a naval base with concrete walls all the way around it. We have sentries at all the gates and walking patrols on the street. They keep nips out and the men in, as it turns out mostly to keep the men in. By the way, I got a nip sword and rifle, I cannot send them home yet but will.

Your brother **Welbie**

#

October 19, 1945
Dear Uncle Bill,

I never wrote you before so I thought I would write. I have three weeks vacation. My teacher is Jean Houghton.

Love **Loretta**

#

October 19, 1945
Dear Billy,

I am expecting you home for Christmas. Donald Kobel got home for the first time in four years and he is awful restless. He had built up in his mind for four years about coming home and when he got here, he was disappointed. Most of the boys that come home that are single reenlist. The radio says they are going back at a thousand a day. I got a letter from Welbie and he said that he and Maurice are together at Yokosuka Japan. Billy Millard is in Japan too.

Lots of love

Your big sister **Eleanor**

#

November 26, 1945

Dear Son,

Grandma is weak and stays in bed most the time. *[Grandma would die a few months after this letter was written.]* Maurice is in the States now; I hope he gets home for Christmas. We took Jean and Mary to Weidman. Jean received four letters from Jack and he talked as if it would not be long before he comes home. Welbie said he would be home in March. Deer are what everyone is talking about now. Roy does not have his yet but Fred got one. Scott is fine. I was hoping all of you boys would be home for Christmas.

Love and God bless

Mom

#

December 14, 1945

Dear Bill,

I am in the Great Lakes Hospital at Great Lakes Illinois and will be here until I get out of the Corp. Welbie is still in Japan and Jack is in China.

Maurice

#

December 29, 1945

Dear Bill,

I am home for Christmas on liberty. Welbie is now in the States in San Francisco. I will be discharged some time in February. Write me at Lee M. Houghton, Ward 1703 N Lawrence, Unit USNH, Great Lakes Illinois.

Love **Maurice**

#

January 3, 1945
Dear Bill,

At long last, I am writing you. I have intended to write you for some time but since Mary received those nice dolls from you, we could not put if off any longer. I am starting a doll collection for her with the ones Jack is sending from China. Maurice is in the hospital at the Great Lakes. He is doing better. Welbie is in San Francisco; Jack is still in China and does not know when he will be home. He dislikes the Chinese as much as the Japs. Your father has his hands full. The new barn is almost finished and the old barn is full of cows. The twelfth calf in a month was just born. Bye for now. Jean and Mary Houghton.

Some of the boys' letters may seem harsh and abrupt, but they have to be taken in context with what they were going through at the time. They spent weeks at a time wondering if their next breath was going to be their last breath. They saw close friends lose body parts and many lose their lives. They had the added stress of worrying about their brothers fighting with them: would they be maimed or killed? On top of that, they had to deal with sleep deprivation, bad weather, bad food, and an enemy that was barbaric and fought to the death.

Stars

1946

During World War II, every family displayed a star in the window of their home for every family member serving in the war. Grandma Houghton had four stars in her window, and those stars had been the focal point of her life for the previous four years. She prayed that each star would shine brightly wherever it was placed, and that its light would never be blown out.

The war was now over, and her stars began to return home. First to return was Lee in February and then William in March. Welbie went to New York to live with his new wife, Betty, and then Jack returned from China.

All of the boys had changed. They seemed older, more mature, with an air of self-confidence. To Grandma, William was the most transformed. He was the youngest of the four and was only seventeen when he left with Welbie on their four-year adventure. Now William was a young man of twenty-one with facial hair, tall and handsome, with a worldly sophistication that only traveling to other cultures can bring.

Now that the war was over it was time to remove the stars from the window. As Grandma was taking down the stars she thought about the many nights she had prayed for their safe return: "Let not my enemies triumph over me and keep my sons out of harm's way." She marveled at how God had been an ever-present comfort to her, and she thanked Him again for the safe return of her boys.

The homecoming was a joyous time. The boys had to readjust to civilian life and things were different. They had been away from home for four years and seen the world. How do you explain war to someone who has never been there? A lot had changed and the biggest change was within them, but as most of their generation did, they adjusted quickly and well.

Now most of the greatest generation, as they are called, is nearly gone. They did their best to keep us free. Many young men of their generation never came home alive. Tens of thousands more came home with parts missing. Many endured the terror of battle without a break for weeks and months on end. Yet they took it all in their stride and readjusted to civilian life as though nothing had ever happened.

All my life, when faced with someone who is of the age and could have fought in WWII, I have asked them if they fought the Germans, or the Japanese. If they fought, they would talk about their experience during WWII and tell me what they did.

I am so proud of them all. I will never forget their exploits and bravery. I will never forget the young men who gave the ultimate sacrifice to keep us free. May God bless them and keep them.

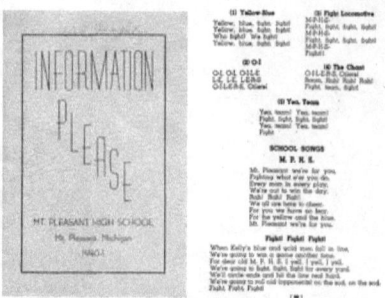

Mt Pleasant, Michigan high school handbook with school cheers, 1940.

William Dale Houghton

William was the fifth of seven children and was born in Detroit, Michigan on September 5, 1924. He had a rough start to his life because as an infant, he contracted pneumonia. Blanche took him to a doctor and the doctor sent her home with the instructions, "Keep him comfortable until he dies." Blanche would not have any of that and called

the women of her church to pray for him. Blanche said the women formed a circle in her living room, placed William in the middle of the circle, and just prayed for him. The prayers of the women and the compassion of a benevolent God came through because William did not die.

To you who answered the call of your country and served in its Armed Forces to bring about the total defeat of the enemy, I extend the heartfelt thanks of a grateful Nation. As one of the Nation's finest, you undertook the most severe task one can be called upon to perform. Because you demonstrated the fortitude, resourcefulness and calm judgment necessary to carry out that task, we now look to you for leadership and example in further exalting our country in peace.

William entered the Marines at the age of seventeen, ended his tour of duty on March 23, 1946, and returned to his parents' farm on Gilmore Road in Mt. Pleasant. Michigan. He was now twenty-one years old. He then farmed with his father for eight years.

One Saturday night while at a dance in Six Lakes, Michigan, he met Viola Eileen Cummings. He asked her for a dance and she said yes. They talked as they danced and William liked what he heard. They spent the night dancing, and as they swayed to the music of a Patti Page song called *Would I Love You*, William listened to the words closely. Patti sang, "Oh for just a chance to love you, would I love you. To take you in my arms has always been my goal. Sure as there's a moon above you, would I love you, with all my heart and soul."

They stayed on the dance floor and continued to dance. The next song was *Because of You*, sung by Tony Bennett:

Because of you there's a song in my heart,

Because of you my romance had its start,

Because of you the sun will shine,

The moon and stars will say you're mine forever and never to part.

I only live for your love and your kiss,

It's paradise to be near you like this,

Because of you my life is now worthwhile,

And I can smile, Because of you.

William didn't know if the music was trying to tell him something, but he knew this night was going to be special, so he saved the ticket stub from the dance, which cost forty cents plus ten cents for tax.

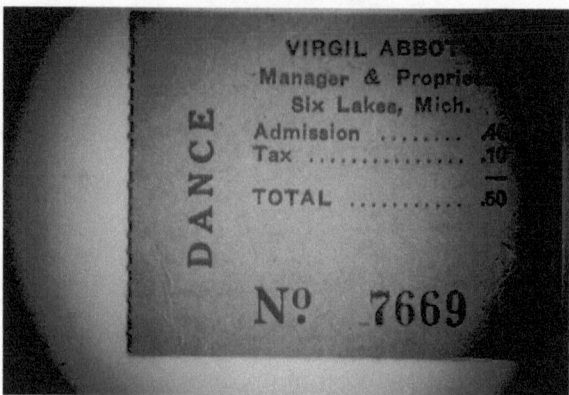

Dance Ticket to Six Lakes, Michigan.

William said that if he ever got married, it would be to Viola (Eileen). They got married on a cool Sunday afternoon on September 30, 1951 at the Methodist Church. It never got warmer than sixty degrees that day.

Niles and Lena Cummings 1919

The Cummings

The other half of my heritage comes from my mother's side of the family, the Cummings. My mother, Viola Eileen Cummings, was born on December 14, 1920.

Viola Eileen Cummings

She was the daughter of Niles A. Cummings, born in Bethany Township, Gratiot County, Michigan on November 3, 1899 and died

February 2, 1998 at the age of ninety-nine years, three months, and twenty-nine days in St. Louis, Michigan. Her mother was Lena B. Rooks, born February 24, 1901 and died April 4, 1992. They are buried at Chapel Gardens Cemetery in

Elwell, Michigan. Niles got his first name from his mother Alida (Lena) Niles' last name. Niles and Lena were married for over seventy years. They lived on a farm outside Breckenridge, Michigan. They had five children: Viola, Jean, Lois, Rex, and Keith.

Niles and Lena gave the following interview to *Midland Daily News* reporter Carol Farrand on their seventieth wedding anniversary.

* * *

Niles and Lena Cummings cannot remember when they did not know each other. It had been almost ninety years since Lena was born just outside Breckenridge, a quarter mile down the road from the farm young Niles and his parents lived on.

Both can remember, however, November 25, 1919—the day Niles married Lena, his childhood companion. "I woke up the day before the wedding," Niles said. "I had a load of sugar beets on a wagon and it was so cold I was afraid they would freeze." Niles proceeded to hitch up his horses and take the load to the mill—a task that proved troublesome. Before he knew it, the horses and load were in the ditch. "A neighbor helped me get out of the ditch with a team of his horses. I persuaded him to take a dollar—a day's wages for a common laborer back then," Niles said. Once he got the load to St. Louis, Niles received four dollars for four tons of beets. When he and his father bought the marriage license, just hours before the ceremony, Niles was left with two dollars in his pocket.

"I don't think anyone ever forgets their courting days," Niles said. "I lived so close to her and teased her all her life, so she had to think about marrying me. I told everyone she had to marry me to get me back for all the teasing I had done to her all her life."

When asked where they went on a honeymoon, Niles replied, "Only the rich went on honeymoons back then. We were only looking for a place with a bed." If Grandma were within earshot of him saying that, he would have gotten an elbow.

After seventy years of marriage, Niles and Lena can see an obvious difference between then and now. Niles is now ninety years old and Lena is eighty-nine years old. "The way we raised our children and the way they are raised today—there is an awful big difference," Lena said.

Niles agreed: "My mother used to worry about me and my horse getting into trouble," he said, laughing. "But after my kids got cars, then I really did have something to worry about."

Niles worked on his farm outside Breckenridge and for Dow Chemical. He loved his horses. He didn't drive a car, so he took the bus to work. I remember the bus stopping in front of the house and Niles getting off the bus. He would walk past the creek and up the drive toward the house. He wore a locomotive hat and bib overhauls, and carried a lunchbox. Lena always did the driving, and that was usually in a Nash automobile.

Niles always had a joke to tell or a song to sing. He was a huge Detroit Tigers fan and I loved to talk to him about the various players they had over the years.

They had the best Bartlett pear trees in their backyard, and in the fall, the children would collect pears from the ground or climb the trees for some pure pear delight and try not to get caught.

Ora and Alida Cummings

Niles was the son of Ora Cummings, born in New York in 1862 and died January 12, 1943. His mother, Alida Niles, was born January 1, 1865 in Alburgh Springs, Vermont. They were married September 10, 1885.

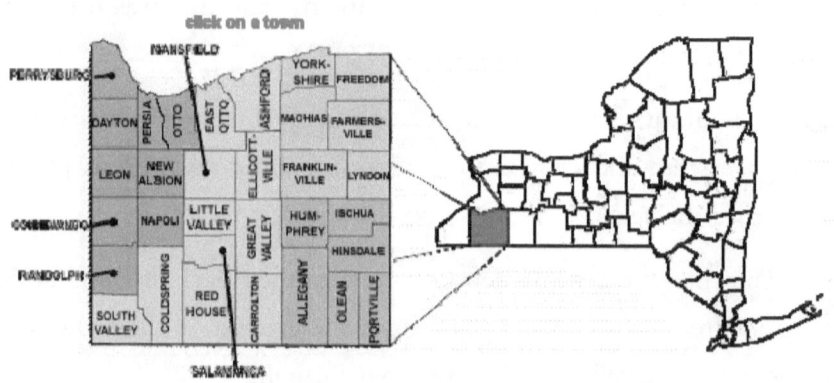

New Albion, New York

Ora was the son of Judson Cummings, born 1846 in New Albion, in the county of Cattaraugus, New York. His mother was Sophrina Sias, also born in New York.

154th New York battle flag.

On September 17, 1864, Judson enlisted in Company B, 154th New York Infantry Regiment. He was placed on the Atlantic and Great Western train and sent south to Atlanta, Georgia to unite with his regiment. The regiment was occupying Atlanta at the time.

He would be involved in ten engagements before mustering out of the army at the end of the war on June 11, 1865 at Bladensburg, Maryland. The following is his timeline of involvement in the Union Army:

1.   Enlisted at New Albion, New York, on September 17, 1864 and took the Atlantic and Western train to Chattanooga Tennessee to Atlanta, Georgia.

2.   Occupation of Atlanta, September to November 15, 1864.

3.   Expedition from Atlanta to Tuckum's Crossroads, October 26-29.

4.   Near Atlanta, November 9, 1864.

5.   March to the Sea, November 15 – December 10, 1864.

6.   Siege of Savannah, December 10-21.

7.   Campaign of the Carolinas, January – April 1965.

8.   Averysboro, North Carolina, March 16, 1865.

9.   Battle of Bentonville, March 19-21, 1865.

10.   Occupation of Goldsboro, March 24, 1865.

11.   Advance on Raleigh, April 13-19, 1865.

12.   Occupation of Raleigh, April 20, 1865.

13.   Bennett's House, April 26, 1865.

14.   Surrender of General Johnston and his army, April 29, 1865.

15.   March to Washington, D.C. via Richmond, VA, May 19, 1865.

16.   Grand review, May 24, 1865.

Nearly a fifth of the regiment died during the war and ninety-four men died as prisoners of war at Andersonville and Richmond. During the Campaign of the Carolinas on February 8 and 9, Judson was treated for neuralgia and was released to duty with no additional record of disability.

A soldier of the 154th New York became famous after the battle of Gettysburg, and his name was Amos Humiston. He was the Unknown Soldier whose dead body was found near the center of Gettysburg after the battle in July 1863. There were no identification papers found on him, only an ambrotype (picture) of his three small children.

He was apparently wounded and then crawled to a secluded place on the battlefield and pulled out the picture of his children, looking at it until he bled to death. The gravediggers found his body with the picture clutched in his hand, took the picture, and marked his grave in hopes of finding his identity from the picture. Newspaper articles were written about the Unknown Soldier and circulated in the North, and hundreds of copies of the photograph were made and distributed.

Finally, in November of the same year, Philenda Humiston heard about the article and asked for a copy of the picture. When she received the

letter with the picture inside, she immediately recognized her children—
Franklin, Alice, and Fredrick—and knew that her husband was dead.

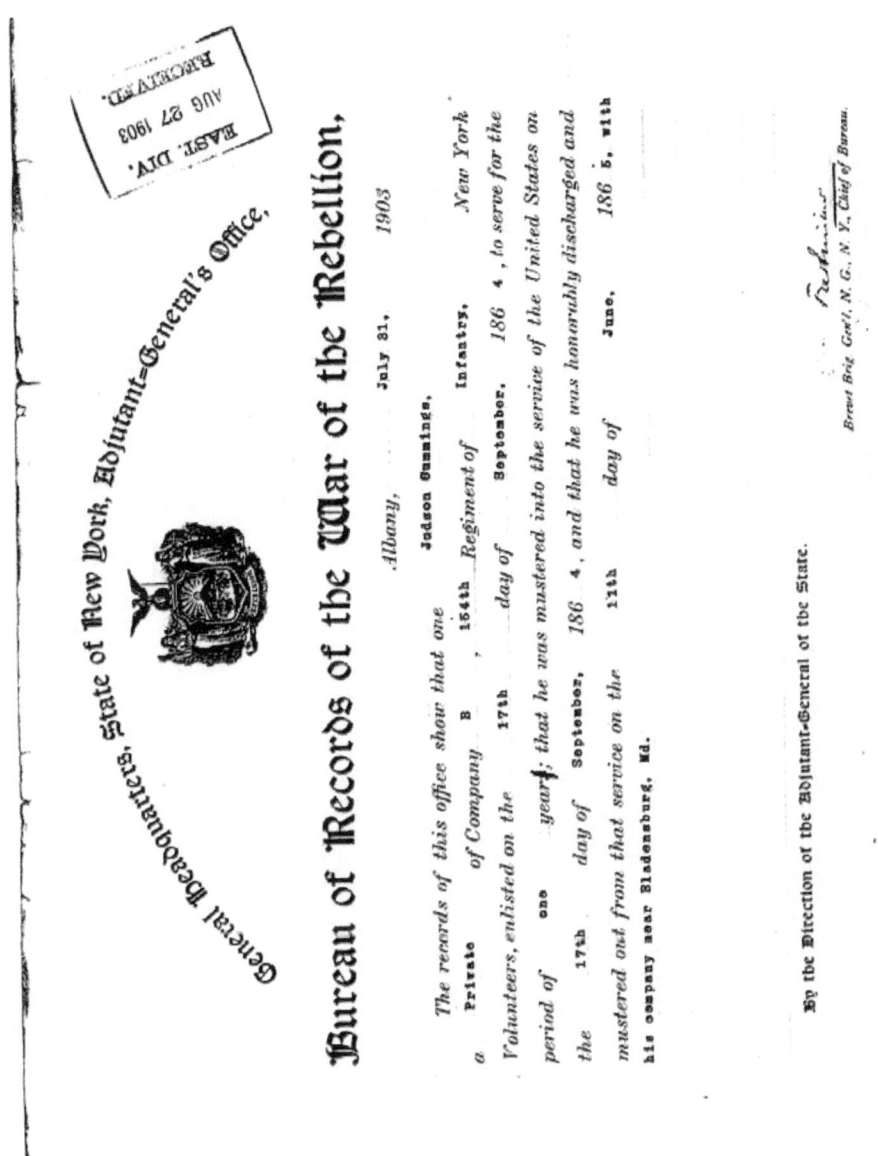

Judson Cummings certificate of service. Civil War.

1860 Census New Albion New York. William, Judson Cummings.

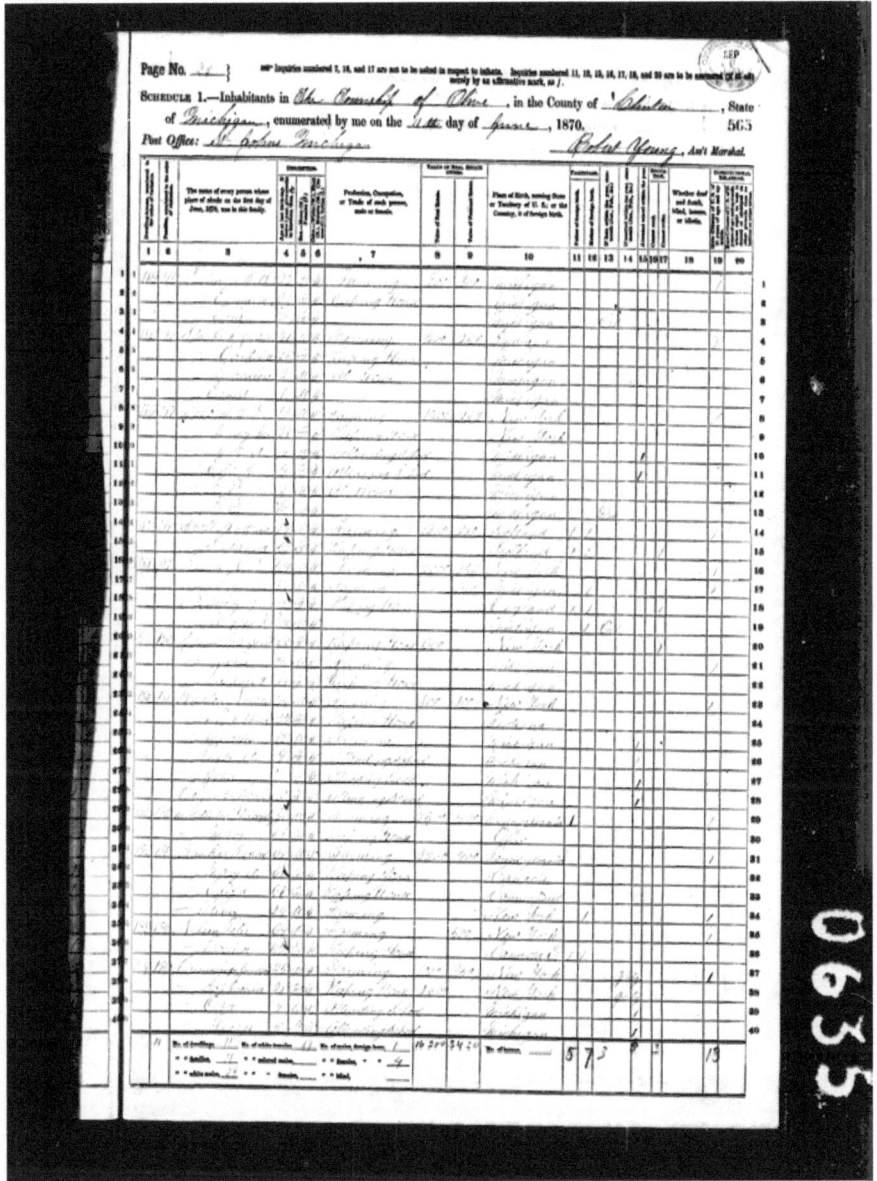

Clinton County, Michigan 1870 census. Judson Cummings.

1880 Census Gratiot County, Michigan, Pine River, Judson and Sophrina Cummings.

The Gratiot Co. Imperial Atlas of 1901, Index of Landowners shows Judson owning land in Section One.

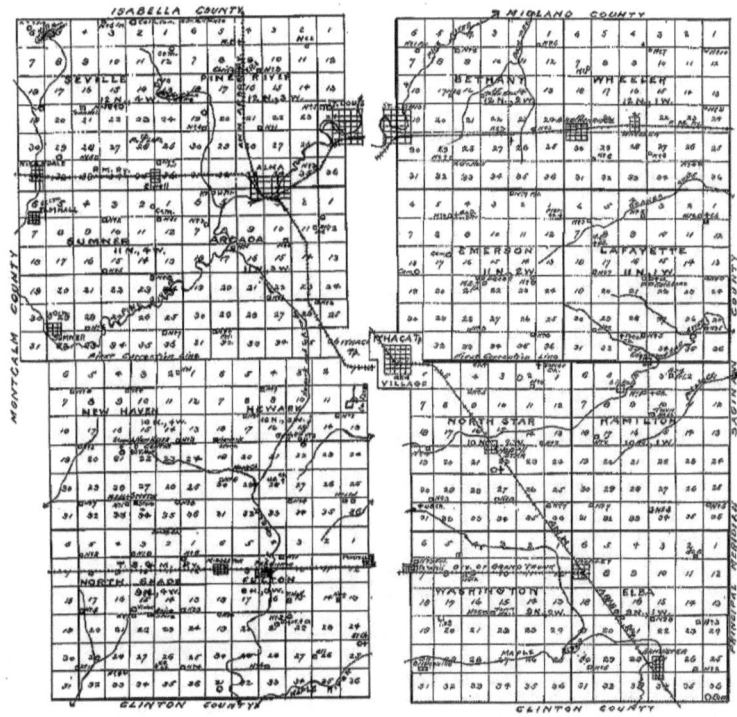

After the war, Judson married Sophrina Sias (born 1841), who was the widow of Judson's uncle. They had five children together, and sometime before 1870, Judson moved the family to Michigan. They were living in the township of Olive in the county of Clinton, Michigan during the 1870 census. By the 1880 census, Judson had moved the family to the Pine River Township near St. Louis, Michigan. Sophrina died on July 12, 1889 at the age of forty-nine and is buried at Oak Grove Cemetery in St. Louis, Michigan.

Judson married Mary A. Adams (Countryman) on January 22, 1897. They were married in Ithaca, Michigan by justice of the peace James G. Kress. Judson was now fifty-one years old and Mary was forty-one. They had one child together named Earl Wade Cummings, born December 21, 1898.

Mary had been married to a John Adams before marrying Judson. They got divorced on July 16, 1895 after having two children together, William P. and James Arthur Adams. John got custody of both children because Mary was found guilty of extreme cruelty and found to be unsuitable to have custody of minor children.

Judson and Mary were married six years when Judson died of heart disease without medical attention on March 3, 1903 at the age of sixty-two. He is buried in lot 168 of the old part, sub one, at Oak Grove Cemetery in St. Louis, Michigan next to his wife Sophrina. The wrong year of birth for Judson was placed on the death certificate and had to be resolved by sworn depositions from Judson's brother William and his sister Anne in 1908.

Also buried at Oak Grove Cemetery in lot 282—old parts across the road from Judson—are his parents, William S. Cummings (1821-1883) and Lydia (Woodmancy) Cummings (May 17, 1824 – October 3, 1906).

Mary was eligible for a pension from the government as a Civil War veteran's widow and received twelve dollars a month for herself and two dollars a month for her minor son Earl W. Cummings.

Mary married Andrew Coon one year after the death of Judson, on March 17, 1904. This would begin a sixteen-year battle with Mary and the government over her pension. Mary was not eligible for the pension for herself if she remarried; only her minor son would get the pension until he reached the age of sixteen.

Mary divorced Andrew Coon on December 13, 1906 because he was an adventurer and refused to provide a living for her. He divorced her on the grounds of desertion. Before Coon divorced Mary, he married another woman and was arrested for bigamy.

Mary married another Civil War veteran named Henry H. Worden on August 21, 1910, but after three stormy months of marriage, she divorced him on the grounds of extreme cruelty and nonsupport.

Mary continued to battle with the government to get her pension back. She was receiving two dollars a month for Earl but only until he reached the age of sixteen. Mary got an attorney who worked on her case pro bono and even enlisted the help of her member of Congress, but with no success—she was not eligible for the pension.

On September 8, 1916, Congress passed the Remarried Widows Pension Act, and Mary saw an opportunity to get her pension money back with the use of this new act of Congress. She was rejected this time because she was found 50% at fault for the divorce from Mr. Worden.

Judson's brother, William W. Cummings, who had been living in Niagara Falls, New York but was now in Vestaburg, Michigan, gave sworn deposition to a special examiner for the Department of the Interior, Bureau of Pensions placed on Mary's case. He testified that

Judson was his brother and that they grew up together, and that Judson joined the Union Army on September 17, 1864. He received a letter from Judson while he was in the war in 1864 or 1865. He sent the letter to the commissioner as evidence. He testified that Earl W. Cummings was Judson's son. Judson's sister, Anna Eliza Watts (Cummings), gave sworn testimony as well that Judson was a Civil War veteran and that Earl was Judson's son.

The following letter is Mary's last desperate plea for the government to take care of her. She handwrites the letter and I have typed it out to make it legible, but I did not change any of the spelling or grammar.

[MARY'S LETTER]

Dear Sirs March 20, 1921

You told me some time ago that thay was a mend coming in the pension work which I would be entitled to a pension and I have not hird frome thare since now through the helps of the grate god.

If thay is any thing you can do for me let me know.

I sopose some of you people are having grate good times nearly all your life.

Whare I have been for fiftey years waring out my life working veary hird.

Wore out frome work and troubel

Never went to school one day in my life to lirn and I want to till you the goverment is to blame for it

Now I will till you why

Long years ago my poor father had to pay three hundred dolars which took his fairm. Then us children had to tirn in and work hird to pay for another farm and help to earn our liveing.

Now you may say like some others why dident he go to war.

I can till you why because he had to stay at home and take care of my sickley mother and three little ones and when he paid this money out he was told that he would get in back some day and entres and some years ago a man read in the news paper that the law was pased and the govner sined it that these men was to get that money back and now as near as I know thay are all ded now.

If it had not been for my children and me

my poor father would of died in the country house

But we took care of him and baryed him.

Now you may say why dont my children take care of me.

Now I will till you because thay all have famelyes and are poor

Some of them poor health.

Now please dont think that every body had thar life easy because some of you did.

I hope you will excuse my poor writing but I dont beleve you will find any one that can do any better for what chance I have had.

I have had non at all.

Only through will power and practes.

Now I am looking to the goverment for my suport what little time I live.

I am now a bout fiftey 7 seven years of age.

My life about ware out frome hird work and the goverment to blame.

I stirted to work hird on a fairm since I was 7 seven years of age and when my poor father became old and helples I took care of him and helped to bary him which the goverment should don and I had all the care of my poor solder husband 7 seven year until he died.

He had poor health all that time

His name was Judson W Cummings

7 seventeen years ago I bared him the 3 of march he died

Now I have nothing to help my self.

I have had to depend on the mircey of my good naybors this winter.

And it is so hird for me to write as hird as a days work.

I wish you would let the present see this letter.

veary truley

Mrs Mary A Cummings

Ovid Mich

March 20, 1921,

Dear Sir you told me
some time ago that thay
was a mend coming in the
Pension work which I would
Be Entitled to a Pension
and I have not hird frome
thare Since now through
the helpe of the grate god
if thay is any thing you
can do for me let me know
Be for Some of you people
are having grate good times
nearly all your life whare
I have been for fifty years
woring out my life working
very hird wore out frome
work and trubel never
went to school one day in
my life to lirn and I want
to till you the goverment is
to blame for it now

will till you why; long
years ago my poor father
had to pay three hundred
dolars which took his
farm then we children
had to tirn in and work
hard to pay for another
farm and help to earn
our liveing now you may
say like some others why
dident he go to wardcan
till you why; because he
had to stay at home and
take care of my sickley
mother and three little
ones and when he paid
this money out he was
told that he would get
it back some day and
entres and some years
ago a man read in the
newr paper that the
law was pased and

the govner fixed it that
there men was to get
that money back and
now as near as I know
thay are all ded now
if it had not been for
my children and me
my poor father would
of died in the country
house but we took care
of him and baryed him
now you may say why
dont my children take
care of me now I will
till you because thay
all have famelyes and
are poor some of them poor
health now please dont
think that everybody
had thay life easy
because some of you did
I hope you will excuse
my poor writing but I

don't beleve you will
find anyone that can
do any better for what
chance I have had I have
had non utall only
through will Power
and piractes now I am
looking to the goverment
for my suport what little
time I live I am now a
bout fiftey seven years
of age my wife about wore
out froine hird work and
the goverment to blame I
stirted to work hird on
a faivm since I was seven
years of age and when
my poor father became
old and helples I took
care of him and helped
to bary hem which the
goverment should don
and I had all the care of

my poor soldier husband
Theren year untill he
died he had poor health
all that time his name
was Judson W

Cummings

7 Seventeen years ago I
bared him the 3 of march
he died now I have nothing
to help my self I have
had to depend on the
mircey of my good naybors
this winter and it is so
hird for me to write
as hird as a days work
I wish you would let
these present see this
Letter veary truley
Mrs Mary W Cummings
Ovid
Mich

please send this
card back to me

William

Gary, Dennie, Jeanie, Roxanne.

Gary and Welbie.

Welbie on horse and Dennie.

William and Eileen Houghton

1951-1955

William and Eileen spent the first four years living on the Houghton farm. William farmed the first three years with Grandpa but eventually took a job at Lobdale Emmery in Alma, Michigan in 1954. They lived next door to William's sister Elaine, her family, and Grandpa and Grandma Houghton.

Eileen had two boys, Gary Lee and Dennis Emory Holton, from a previous marriage. The last name was so similar to "Houghton" that when the family moved to Shepherd and the boys started going to school, the teachers thought the boys were misspelling their last name.

Viola, Dennie and Gary.

Three children would be added to the family while William and Eileen were living on the farm. The first was Welbie Dale (myself), the second was Vanessa Eileen, and the third was James William.

Gary and Dennie tell a story about an event that happened while they were living on the farm. They were watching me one day and put me in a stroller. They strolled me out to the barn and were racing me back and forth in the middle of the barn on the cement floor. There were stalls along the sides where cows would stand to be milked. Troughs were built into the floor the length of the barn at the end of the stalls that took care of the excrement from the cows.

On one pass down the middle of the barn, the stroller overturned and I went flying headfirst down the trough of excrement. I was covered from head to toe with pie, cow pie. Gary and Dennie used my pajamas to clean me up, and in their panic to hide the evidence, put the pajamas in William's fishing tackle box and forgot about it. That fall when William was preparing for a fishing trip, he opened his fishing tackle box to discover a pair of crusty pajamas.

Welbie, Vanessa, William, and Jim Houghton, 1955.

Welbie Vanessa Jim

HOUGHTON FAMILY ALBUM
1792 - 1992.

Gary Dennie

DVD ONE

Shepherd, Michigan

1955-1976

William and Eileen moved to 205 Orchard Ave, Shepherd, Michigan in the fall of 1955. Shepherd was a sleepy little farming community where everyone knew everyone else's business. The town was founded in 1857 and the family was there to experience the one-hundred-year centennial.

Most people who lived in Shepherd commuted to other towns for employment, and the largest employer was the public school. The town had a couple of grocery stores but most people drove to Mt.

Pleasant to get their groceries. Shepherd had a dime store, but that closed in the late sixties. There was a bank, a pharmacy, a barbershop, a local restaurant called the Kitchenette—which we lived directly behind—and two gas stations, and not much else. The movie theater had closed before we moved there.

I attended school there grades K through 12. I walked the same path to school for thirteen years—through the back yard, downtown, and then through several neighborhoods until I reached the school. It was always a cold walk in the winter, a wet walk when it rained, and a dry, warm walk when the sun was shining.

Shepherd hundred-year centennial-Front row: Welbie, Vanessa, Jim Back row: Dennie, Gary

Other than a new high school building, very little changed at the school during the thirteen years I went there. I was fortunate enough to live in the same house in the same town and attend the same school with the same schoolmates for the entire thirteen years.

One event that many children participated in was the collection of sap from the many maple trees throughout Shepherd. All the trees in the town that were twenty years old or older would be tapped with a spigot, and a bucket was hung from the spigot. The sap from the maple tree would run from the spigot into the bucket. It is surprising that any tree could afford to lose so much of its natural nourishment without dying, but maple trees that have been tapped for fifty years or more seem just as luxuriant in their foliage as those that are untouched.

At the end of the school day, a tractor pulling a large vat would go up and down the streets collecting sap from the trees. The children would collect the buckets and pour the sap into the moving vat as it made its way up the street. The sap was then taken to a boiling-house and boiled down to make maple syrup. It usually took thirty gallons of sap to make one gallon of maple syrup, and each tree was capable of giving ten to fourteen gallons of sap each year.

In the spring, usually the last week of April, the community would have a maple syrup festival. The festival was held to raise money for a community swimming pool at the high school. They would sell pancake meals and maple syrup. All those years of work on the sap wagon, and I never did see that swimming pool.

Crime was almost unheard-of in the town, and it was safe enough for children to play outside all night during the summer. It was the baby boom era, so there were always enough people to form a baseball game or football game.

Television was new but provided only three channels—if you were lucky and had a good antenna. Everything was in black and white, and television only had programming until one o'clock in the morning, then there was a test pattern on the screen until morning. Our TV set usually blew a tube early every summer and would not get fixed until fall. That was okay because we usually played outside with the other children on the block anyway.

There was a big park downtown, and that is where you would go to play shuffleboard or get a baseball game going. It was also the place to go in the summer if you wanted to go swimming. Shepherd did not have a community pool, but if you had fifty cents and a towel, you could catch a bus at the park once a week that would take you to a community pool in St. Louis. To this day, I think of that community pool whenever I hear a song that was regularly played there.

William and Eileen became involved in Amway in 1963 and got the rest of the family involved as well. It was always a great day during the summer if it was your turn to ride with Mom to Ada, Michigan to pick up product because you always got to eat out. Eating out was not something most families did in the fifties and sixties, so it was a huge treat, and well worth sitting in a van for hours.

Dad smoked Little King Edward cigars until I was in high school. This is how small and trusting Shepherd was and how times have changed: Dad would write a note on any scrap of paper, saying, "Please sell my son Welbie a pack of Little King Edwards," and sign it. He would give me the note and money to pay for the cigars and send me to the pharmacy. I would walk downtown to the pharmacy, owned by the Gilsons, and give Mr. Gilson the note and money, and he would give me the cigars.

Winter was always a lot of fun because the Derrys, our next-door neighbors, would flood their back yard with water and make an ice-skating rink. We would spend hours on the ice, skating until our feet became so numb that we would have to go into the house to suffer the torment of feeling returning to our feet. There were always plenty of outdoor activities to keep everyone busy.

We would pray often for a large snowstorm so school would be called off, and after a big snowstorm all the children close to the Kitchenette would hurry over to their parking lot and begin shoveling the snow. All who did would receive the most delicious donut known to kid-dom.

The Lord is my shepherd I shall
not want.
He maketh me to lie down in green
pastures; he leadeth me beside
the still waters.
He restoreth my soul; he leadeth
me in the paths of righteousness,
for his name's sake.
Yea, though I walk through the
valley of the shadow of death, I will
fear no evil; for thou art with me; thy
rod and thy staff they comfort me.
Thou preparest a table before me in
the presence of mine enemies; thou
anointest my head with oil; my
cup runneth over.
Surely goodness and mercy shall
follow me all the days of my life,
and I will dwell in the house of
the Lord for ever.   *Psalm 23*

In Memory Of
Blanche M. Houghton

Aug. 2, 1892 - Mar. 20, 1968

Place And Time Of Services
Stinson Funeral Home
Sat., March 23, 2 P.M.

Clergyman
Rev. Arlo Vandlen

Interment
Riverside Cemetery
Mount Pleasant, Michigan

Grandmother Blanche Houghton

One of the many things I loved about Grandmother Houghton was her ability to make you feel like she was giving you her complete, undivided attention when you were with her. That always made me feel special.

There were many things to do at her home. She lived on a large farm, and there were many places to explore. The big barn was a personal favorite, especially when it was full of cows and pigs. We could play for hours in the hayloft. When we were exploring the farm, we always had to keep a watchful eye out for the tom turkey. He was territorial and would not hesitate to run you off if you invaded his space.

Grandma's kitchen smelled of apples, and I loved her apple pie and applesauce. In the summer, we would make homemade ice cream and everyone would take turns cranking the ice-cream churn.

Grandma seldom forgot your birthday, and that was no small accomplishment considering all the relatives she had to remember. When my birthday came around, Grandma and Grandpa would drive over to our house in their big Lincoln Continental. They would visit for a while, then Grandma would open her purse and pull out a birthday envelope. She would call me over to her, say happy birthday, and give me the envelope with a big kiss and hug. Inside the envelope were always two brand-new one-dollar bills. Two dollars was a small fortune to me because you could buy twenty packs of Tops baseball cards. Each pack contained five baseball cards and one large piece of the best chewing gum in the land. Two dollars meant twenty pieces of gum and one hundred baseball cards. Grandma was always a safe place to land and she loved you unconditionally.

March 20, 1968 was a cold rainy Wednesday that was filled with sadness for me; Grandma Houghton passed away that day. There were many firsts involved with this day; this was the first death of someone I knew personally, the first time I realized that death comes to us all, and the first time I saw my father cry uncontrollably. My dad and mom explained what had happened to Grandma and what was going to happen as far as the funeral was concerned. I was allowed to stay home from school that day and spent most of the day in my bedroom trying to make sense of death.

I attended the funeral on Saturday, March 23 and saw all of my aunts, uncles, and cousins there. Ordinarily this would have meant a great time was in store except for the fact that this was a funeral. I sat somewhere in the middle of the crowd of people at the funeral, and my dad sat in the front with his brothers, sisters, and father.

Grandma's casket was open and she looked so peaceful, just like she was sleeping. At first I couldn't believe she was dead. I thought perhaps they made a mistake, and she was only sleeping and could not open her eyes. I watched her body intensely throughout the funeral for any signs of life. I closed my eyes and pleaded with God, "If you let Grandma live, I promise I will be good and never do another bad thing as long as I live." I opened my eyes and watched for a breath. To my amazement, I saw Grandma take a breath. I thought that my heart was going to beat out of my chest; couldn't anyone else see what I saw? I looked around the funeral parlor at everyone there and no one seemed to notice her breathing. Then I began to wrestle with myself, should I stand up and say something? I continued to watch and as I did, I realized it was the wishful thinking of a young boy who did not want to say good-bye to his grandmother. Blanche was buried at Riverside Cemetery in Mt. Pleasant, Michigan.

Grandfather John III Donald Houghton

I could not attend the funeral of Grandfather John IV Houghton because I was in the military at the time, but I remember the day he died well. It was an unusually warm and sunny day for that time of the year.

I remember being summoned to the company commander's office for an urgent meeting. The first sergeant, who was very pompous and not well liked, told me how to address the commander and how to act in his presence. I did not know what to expect when I stepped into the commander's office, my only thoughts were about what I might have done wrong.

I saluted the commander and stood at attention as I waited for him to speak. He told me that my parents had notified the American Red Cross that my Grandfather Houghton had passed away and wanted me to know. The news was a relief that I was not in trouble, but something so unexpected that my emotions hit me like an atomic bomb. As I listened to the commander speak, I struggled not to let him see me cry, but there was no way of holding back the pain the news brought to me. Tears were streaming down my cheeks, and my lower lip was quivering when the commander said, "That is all." I saluted him, did an about face, and walked to the door to leave. As I opened the door to go, I tried in vain to hide the tears so no one else could see that I was crying.

The last day I saw my grandfather was the day before I went into the service. The day Grandpa died, November 7, 1972, was a sad day for me. Grandpa was buried next to Grandma at Riverside Cemetery.

John Donald (1893-1972) and Blanche Mary Houghton (1892-1968).

Got Milk?

One sweltering summer's day when I was nine years old, Dad asked me to get a gallon of milk from Dick's IGA, a local grocery store that was about two blocks downtown. I walked to the store, got the gallon of milk from the cooler, and paid for it.

The cashier did not put the milk in a bag—milk back then came in a glass bottle—and now I was walking in downtown Shepherd with this glass bottle of cold milk in my bare hands. The hot summer sun began to shine on the bottle and it began to sweat, and the more it sweated, the more slippery it got. With every step I took, it became more difficult to handle, so I thought I would set the bottle down and warm and dry my hands for a better grip. When I set the cold glass bottle of milk on the scorching-hot cement sidewalk, it burst and milk started flowing down the street.

I began to panic. I could image that the worst spanking I had ever received was now in store for me when I got home. I thought of running away from home… but where would I go? I could say someone bumped into me and made me drop the bottle—no, I didn't want to lie. A dozen different scenarios went though my mind as I slowly walked back home, but I knew I had to tell the truth.

I walked into the house through the back door and went to the kitchen, where my parents were busy making supper. Before I could tell them what had happened, I started to cry as if I had already gotten my spanking. Through the tears and gasping for breath, I told them the whole story. I braced for the worst, but my dad said, "It's okay," and took me by the hand and we started walking back to the grocery store. When we came to the broken milk bottle still lying on the sidewalk, we stopped and picked up the broken glass and threw it away. We walked into the store and I stood to the side as my dad talked to the owner of the store. The owner apologized for not giving me a bag for the milk and gave us a free replacement bottle of milk. This time the milk was placed in a bag and my dad gave the bag to me to carry home.

The simple act of giving me the bag to carry said volumes to me: Dad trusted me. As we walked home, we didn't talk about anything that had to do with the milk. I remember talking about my Little League team, the Lions, and going to the county fair. I loved my dad, but that day I really loved him.

When we walked past the spilled milk on the sidewalk I began to laugh to myself—I had worried for nothing. We walked home and just before we went into the house, an old saying came to mind: "Don't cry over spilled milk." And you know, they were right.

Vanessa and Welbie at Horsehead Lake.

Camping

We often went camping when I was growing up, sometimes in a tent, mostly in a travel trailer, but there was a log cabin on Horsehead Lake my parents rented a few times that I remember the most.

It was a rustic cabin with no modern amenities. It was a great place for a young boy, a place where I learned to fish, catch frogs and fireflies, and let my imagination run free.

The air was always ablaze with sounds: shrill sounds and muted sounds, soothing sounds and aimless sounds. Sounds that only the imagination of a young boy could hear: growls of the world's largest mountain lion in flight from the world's greatest boy hunter, screams of bloodthirsty savages coming to ransack our cabin and carry us all away.

The cabin was a place of enchantment where all the dreams of a young boy could come true if only he believed; where I learned many lessons about nature and a place I will always remember with great affection.

How to eat a whale

I have traveled to thirty-two countries on five continents and have been involved in a lot of red tape to enter a county, but the entry to West Germany was one of the easiest I ever made. Now to find our hosts at the airport, forty-five minutes went by and no one. I had the information booth at the airport announce through the PA system that the forward edge team had arrived and were waiting in the lobby. Finally, someone greeted us; they said, "We were looking for a much younger team." Our response was, "We were younger when we left, it was a long flight."

There were eleven of us from Northern Michigan, ranging in age from twenty-eight to seventy-three. The team comprised of eleven ordinary people without any titles, just a call on their lives to go to Eastern Europe and share the good news of Jesus Christ. If we were to be given a title, I guess you could call us "Christians in training". Only three of us had ever been on a missions' trip before. What we lacked in experience, we made up with enthusiasm, determination, and complete dependence on God.

We spent four months before the trip meeting in prayer, training, and getting comfortable with one another. God used those four months knitting us together as a team.

Now we were in Munich, West Germany, eager to put to use what we had learned. (West Germany and East Germany were still separate countries then.) We spent two days in orientation in Munich. Then we drove north through West Germany to the border of East Germany. We were detained at the East German for two hours. We had to obtain visas to get through the country and all our belongings had to be searched by the boarder guards. After acquiring our visas, we set out east along the bottom of E. Germany to the border with Poland. Again, we had another extended wait to get through customs. The Lord was preparing us for the long lines we would experience in Poland. We saw lengthy lines of cars waiting for gas at gas stations as we drove to Legnica, Poland. There were lines everywhere for mostly everything. I was told that it wasn't as bad as it used to be, but I stood in line at a bank for two hours to exchange money, and another line for one hour at a grocery store to get food. The best time to get gasoline was three a.m. because the lines would be the shortest.

The people in Poland were hungry for the gospel. There was so little to be happy about. Most of their lives were spent taking care of their daily needs. They were hungry for some good news. We had the good news they were searching for and we knew it. We wanted to make the most of our time there. That's why we went to the streets and parks of Legnica, Wroclaw, Jawaor, Poland two and three times a day. We sang and preached the love of God and of his son Jesus Christ. We told everyone who would listen that God was personally present in Christ, reconciling and restoring the world to favor with Himself, not counting up and holding men's sins against them, but canceling them. We handed out 5,000 tracts in Poland to people who were so hungry for the good news that they came to us for tracts. We would move from one area of the town to another and people would follow us. Many people gave their hearts to Jesus every day.

I had a vision one day while in prayer. In the vision, I saw hundreds of people standing before us listening to what we had to say. In the chest of many of the people who were listening was a black spot where the heart was supposed to be. As we sang and shared the word of God, arrows of light came forth from our mouths. The arrows were like heat sensitive missiles that headed directly for those darkened hearts and pierced them. Those hearts would turn in color from black, to gray, then white as more and more arrows of light penetrated them. Then the person's countenance would change and they would give their life to Christ.

We saw the power of praise and worship as we focused our attention upon God and Him only. As we worshipped and praised his mighty name, God would send large crowds to us to minister to. All we had to do was be sensitive to His leading and speak the words He was giving us for all those divine appointments He was arranging.

We learned something of value the first day on the streets. Just as the raised arms of Moses meant victory for the Israelites in their battle against the Amlekites, so too praise and worship meant the difference between being effective or ineffective. We had six or seven people engaged in praise and worship while we were on the streets ministering. If we did not have the praise and worship, the crowds would leave and people would not receive our tracts.

After five fruitful days in Poland, we drove to Nordhaussen, E. Germany. There we spent only two days, but it was two days I will never forget. The pastor we were staying with in Nordhaussen was a member of the underground church. After the Berlin Wall came down the church became public and had been unrestricted for seven months. The public schools in E. Germany were forced to teach a communism class before the falling of the wall. Now they no longer had to do this and there was freedom to explore other ideas. The public schools asked the mainline denominational churches in Nordhaussen to fill this open class: "Tell the children about God," they asked. However, the churches refused, stating, "There should be separation of church and state." The pastor we were with said he would fill that class.

Six people from my team, plus me, had the opportunity to go with the pastor for his first day in the school. As leader of the team, it was my responsibility to choose the six that would go. Everyone on the team wanted to go to the school, but I could only choose six. At first I began to panic, I did not want to hurt anyone's feelings because this was a huge opportunity. It was late at night and it had been a long day. We got in a circle and began to pray for the school, and after prayer, we were all going to bed for some much-needed sleep for the big day. As we started to pray, the Lord softly said to me, "Listen and you will know who to take tomorrow." One person began to pray, then another, and then another, before we were done praying exactly six people had prayed plus myself. These were the people the Lord had chosen to go to the school the next day.

All schools in E. Germany were renamed after World War II for a famous Russian. The school we were going to was named after the first Russian cosmonaut that flew into space, Yuri Gagarin. Yuri Gagarin made the infamous speech after his flight saying, "I've flown through heaven, and there is no God." He met God face to face seven years later when his plane crashed and he was killed. We had the first class of the day, and it was forty-five minutes long. We actually had one and half hours that morning because the students gave up their breakfast to stay with us. The students were grades nine through twelve, and the small auditorium was full of about 200 students and teachers.

As we stood and began to give testimony of what God had done in our lives, the school administrator began to cry. As I looked out over the auditorium, I saw hankies being pulled from purses and pockets to wipe away tears and dry noses. God was moving by His Spirit on the hearts of those children and teachers. When our time was over, the school administrator, a man in his early forties, stood before the children and apologized to them because they had never been given the opportunity to hear what they heard that morning.

The school administrator then took us back to his office and asked us many questions. We spent and hour answering his questions, and when we were done we gave him a Bible. Twice the administrator's secretary, who would remind him of appointments he had that morning, interrupted us. He would always tell her, "They can wait, I have something more important to discuss."

We told the children that we would be downtown that afternoon signing and speaking, and if they had any questions they could ask us there. One of the young women in the auditorium that morning brought her parents to where we were, and they all gave their lives to Christ.

All of us were in awe because if we had done this seven months earlier, before the Berlin Wall came down, we could have been put in prison.

I could continue with stories of drug addicts, punkers, street people, down-and-outers, up and-comers, and everyday people whose lives have been changed. Changed because eleven ordinary Christians took an extraordinary message to where they were and took the time to get involved in their lives. Not only were the lives of the people we touched changed, but also we can never be the same.

It was only sixteen days but that was a start. How do you eat a whale? The overwhelming size of it seems impossible. The way to eat a whale is ...*One bite at a time.* That's how you change the world, one person at a time. God wants to bless all the nations of the earth through you, Christian. Will you go and be a blessing in Jesus' name?

The Musician

Every family has stories that are embarrassing when the event happens but become downright humorous as time passes. This is one of those stories.

The year was 1968 and I was in the tenth-grade high school band. Every year the band played concerts in the high school gymnasium and all the community was welcome to attend. The concerts always had a large attendance, mainly because they were free and partly because there wasn't anything else to do in Shepherd.

This year my mother, father, younger sister, and brother came to the concert with my nephew Randy and niece Lee Ann, who was five years old. They arrived at the gymnasium early enough to get seats four rows from the stage and exactly in the middle of the row. Every seat in the gym was taken, and some guests had to watch the concert standing in the back.

It was now time for the concert to begin and the curtains opened on the stage, revealing the band. The conductor, Mr. Lemmer, walked onto the stage and up to the podium; he was met with applause. He bowed to the audience and then stepped up on the podium, facing the band. He motioned for the band to watch him as he raised his arms with his baton in his hand, and the music began.

At the end of every song, there was thunderous applause, as if the Boston Philharmonic had just finished playing one of its famous concertos. Mr. Lemmer would bow to the audience and thank them for their appreciation of our magnificent performance and then the same routine would start again. Band members would change their sheet music for the next song, the conductor raised his baton, and boom, the next song would begin.

Earlier in the evening, while we were still at home, we talked to Randy and Lee Ann about being in the band when they got older. Randy said he would like to play the drums and Lee Ann said she would like to play the trumpet.

The night was successfully progressing to the finale, and the band finished playing its fifth song, followed by the usual thunderous applause. The conductor stepped onto the podium and the gymnasium became quiet. The conductor raised his baton to start the next song... and without any warning, there came a loud noise from the audience. You might hear that explosive blast after someone has eaten beans and then washed them down with a beer... and the foul, fetid odor that accompanied it was distinctive.

After the flatulence, everyone in the audience could hear this small but loud voice say, "Grandpa." Lee Ann, my little niece, was sitting next to my father, and when she passed gas, she hit my father and said, "Grandpa," as if he had been the perpetrator of the strident sound.

All eyes were on my father, who was turning four shades of red, and there were several snickers in the audience. Mr. Lemmer, who understood the gravity of the situation, quickly started the next song and the night carried on.

After the concert was over, Lee Ann said that she had just been trying to be part of the concert and played the only instrument she had, her Butt Trumpet.

That's My Story and I'm Sticking to It

This book only briefly touches the multitude of stories the family has. Even if I knew every story there was to tell, I couldn't find a book big enough to hold them. My generation experienced an explosion of growth in family members. I alone had twenty-four aunts and uncles, with forty-four lively cousins. I remember my childhood with fondness, and that is due in part to the fantastic times I had with my relatives while growing up. The many excursions the family embarked upon, the usual gatherings at holidays, and the unusual gatherings we called "cousins' reunion" were always something I looked forward to and will cherish forever.

Now it will be up to the next generation to carry on the tradition of the family and to record its history. Live a happy life and enjoy every day because life jets by so quickly. Time is a cruel taskmaster that respects nothing; it speeds when you could do with more and drags as soon as you require less. At the end of your days, when you stand on top of your mountain of old age and look in the mirror of hindsight, all you will have are the memories.

When you are gone and someone records your deeds, how will you look…

Through their **e**y**e**s?

Thank you for reading my book. If you have any photos or other information you would like to share about my family, please send it to me at minimejr@charter.net

Acknowledgements

I would like to thank my wife, Jane, for her support and encouragement while I was writing this book. She has had to live with the family past for the last two years and could probably tell this story better than I. In addition, I would like to thank relatives and friends who contributed pieces of Houghton information to the family puzzle. Finally yet importantly, I would like to thank my parents, William and Eileen, for all they have contributed to me in my life. I only wish they were alive so I could thank them in person.

The Houghton family tree

Descendants of **William Houghton** b. 1792 in Lincolnshire, England-d. Oct. 13, 1886 at Lynn, Michigan and **Elizabeth Burns** b.____?. m. 1817, d.____ Skegness, Lincolnshire, England.

Generation I.

A, William Houghton b. 1818 in Lincolnshire, England m.____ first wife died in
. England 1851.

B. John Houghton b. July 11, 1824 in Lincolnshire, England. d. Jan. 16, 1906 at Lynn,
Mi. m. Jane Sleight (b. March 20, 1819 in Lincolnshire, England. d. Sep. 17, 1896 at
Lynn) 1845 in Skegness, Lincolnshire, England.

C. Mary b.____ in Lincolnshire, England. Stayed in England with her mother Elizabeth
had one daughter.

Generation II

A. Children of **William II Houghton** and his first Wife:

1a. Maryann b. 1836 in Lincolnshire, England m. John Milligan of Lynn

2a. Betsy b.1839 in Lincolnshire, England m. Mytrot

3a. Rebecca b.1842 in Lincolnshire, England m. Van Dewalker

4a. William b. 1845 in Lincolnshire, England m.___?

5a. Mariah b. 1846 in Lincolnshire, England m. Robert Sterling

Children of **William II** and his second wife.

6a. Richard b.____at Brown City, Michigan

7a. Elizabeth b.____at Imlay City, Michigan

B. Children of **John Houghton** and Jane Sleight:

1b. John II b. May 11, 1846 in Lincolnshire, England d. May 10, 1920; m. Caroline ..
. Wickham (b. Jan. 8, 1855 Sombra, Canada d. 1946) on July 3, 1872 at Lynn.

2b. Eliza b. March 31, 1848 in Lincolnshire, England d. January 10, 1921 at Fairgrove,
. Michigan. m. Steven Stevenson at Brockway, Michigan on Sept. 10, 1866-they ....
. Divorced-later m. Daniel Cartwright at Lynn.

3b. Emma b. 1850 in Lincolnshire, England d.___at Mt. Pleasant, Michigan, m. Daniel
. Maclachlan at Mt. Pleasant.

4b. Ellen b. 1854 in Lynn, Michigan d.____buried at Valley Center, m. Johnathan .....
. Steinhoff.

5b. Jane b. 1856 in Lynn, Michigan d. 1866 at Lynn, Michigan

6b. Richard Henry b. Nov. 24, 1857 d.___at Fairgrove, buried at Lynn, m. Cora
Hollenbeck b. 1858 d.___at Flint, Michigan.

7b. Elizabeth (Lizzie) b. 1861 at Lynn, Michigan d.1904 at Lynn, Michigan, m. Robert
Shutt

Generation III

1a Children of **Mary Ann Houghton** and John Milligan:
1a1 John
1a2 William
1a3 Janette
1a4 Mariah
1a5 Eva, daughter of Betsy, adopted by Mary Ann

2a Children of Betsy Houghton and ____Mytrot,
1b1 Eva b___adopted by Mary Ann.
Children of Rebecca Houghton and ___Van Dewalker, not known.
Children of William III, not known.
Children of Mariah Houghton and Robert Sterling, not known.
Children of Richard Houghton not known.
Children of Elizabeth Houghton not know.

1b Children of **John II Houghton** and Caroline Wickham:
1b1 Andrew b. August 13, 1873 at Lynn, Michigan, d. November 7, 1873
1b2 Catherine Jane (Katie) b. September 11, 1874 at Lynn, Michigan, m. Sylvester R. Baughman at Mt. Pleasant, Michigan. They had no children. Later married Frank A. Worthington at Shepherd in 1924.
1b3 Ruby E. b. December 17, 1876 at Lynn, Michigan, m. Lester Drew who died and later married Charles Gray a railroad engineer in Winnipeg, Canada.
1b4 Anna Elizabeth b. December 22, 1879 at Lynn, Michigan. m. Parker Atwell at Mt Pleasant, Michigan and moved to Grove City Pennsylvania.
1b5 Maud Caroline b. August 7,1884, at Mecosta, Michigan, m. Fred George Ellis at Winnipeg, Ontario, Canada.
1b6 John III Donald b. January 5, 1893, at Mt. Pleasant, Michigan, d. November 7, 1972 at Mt. Pleasant, Michigan, m. Blanche Mary Taylor (b. August 2, 1893 at Winn, Michigan, d. March 20,1968 at Mt. Pleasant.) Both buried at Riverside Cemetery in Mt. Pleasant, Michigan.

2b Children of **Eliza Houghton** and Steven Stevenson
2b1 Walter E. b. July 21, 1867 at Lynn, Michigan. Raised by John and Jane Houghton.
  Walter became a Presbyterian minister. m. Della___.
Children of Eliza Houghton and Fred Meade Cartwright
  2b2 Fred Daniel b. November 12, 1875 at Gilford, m. Bessie Graham
  2b3 Louis Ezra b. July 23, 1876 at Gilford, Michigan, m. Jessie Green
  2b4 William Houghton b. February 6, 1880 at Gilford, Michigan, m. Blanche Viola Northrip.
  2b5 Alice Bessie b. August 20, 1882 m. David Otto at Fairgrove, Michigan.
  2b6 Ethel May b. December 8, 1888 at Fairgrove, Michigan, m. Henry Pelton on February 2, 1904

4b Children of **Ellen Houghton** and Jonathon Steinhoff
4b1 Mabel b.___

6b Children of **Richard Henry** and Cora Hollenbeck
6b1 Herbert John b. July 9, 1885 at Lynn, Michigan, m. Janet Cameron at Lynn, who died 1920. They had no children. Herbert later married Adella Hazard, they also had no children.
6b2 Sarah Jane (Sadie) b. December 15, 1888 at Lynn, Michigan. m. Robert Martin at Yale on January 5, 1910

Generation IV

Catherine Jane Houghton had no children.
1b3 Children of **Ruby E. Houghton** and Lester Drew
1b31 Arnold
Children of **Ruby E. Houghton** and Charles Gray
1b32 Helen Caroline b. 1914, m. James Master in Winnipeg, Canada.
1b4 Children of **Anna Elizabeth Houghton** and Parker Atwell
1b41 Stewart
1b42 Ross Lincoln
1b43 Wayne Ellis
1b44 John Houghton
1b45 Mary Jane
1b46 Donald
1b47 Ruth
Maud Houghton had no children.
1b6 Children of **John IV Donald Houghton** and Blanche Mary Taylor.
1b61 Eleanor Loretta b. October 30, 1915 at Mt. Pleasant, Michigan, d. September 12,1992, m. Leroy Nelson on October 13, 1933 at Mt. Pleasant, Michigan.
1b62 John V. Donald Houghton b. October 30, 1916 at Mt. Pleasant, Michigan. d. April 12, 2007 m. Jean Sparks August 1943.
1b63 Lee Maurice b. September 1918 at Mt. Pleasant, Michigan, m. Eugenia (Jean) Janus February 1946.
1b64 Welbie Elton b. October 21, 1920 at Hillman, Michigan, m. Betty Clark at Ithaca, New York August 1944
1b65 William Dale b. September 44, 1924 in Detroit, Michigan d. May 9, 1996, m. Viola Eileen Cummings on September 21, 1951 at Mt. Pleasant, Michigan.
1b66 Blanche Elaine b 1928 in Detroit, Michigan, m. Richard Wood 1946
1b67 Kenneth Scott b. August 27, 1935 in Mt. Pleasant, Michigan, m. Donna Lieter in August 1954.

Generation V

Children of **Eleanor Houghton** and Leroy Nelson
1. **Loretta**
2. **Leroy II**

Children of **John IV Houghton** and Jean Sparks
1. Mary
2. Nora
3. John V
4. Janet
Children of **Lee Houghton** and Eugenia Janus
1. Lynn
2. Lee II
3. Brian
Children of **Welbie Houghton** and Betty Clark
1. Daya
2. William
3. Joy
4. John
Children of **William Houghton** and Viola Cummings
1. Gary
2. Dennis
3. Welbie
4. Vanessa
5. James
Children of **Blanche Houghton** and Richard Wood
1. Roxanne
2. Cathy
3. Richard II
4. Timothy
5. Jeff
Children of **Kenneth Houghton** and Donna Lieter
1. Katie
2. Kelley
3. Kenneth
4. Karrie

www.ingramcontent.com/pod-product-compliance
Lightning Source LLC
Chambersburg PA
CBHW061348280526
45784CB00001B/177